SHERROD VILLAGE

a memoir

Barbara Williams Lewis, Ph.D.

MORPH PUBLISHING
ROUND ROCK, TEXAS

Morph Publishing
P.O. Box 1235
Round Rock, Texas 78680-1235

PRINT: 978-0-9903989-0-5
EBOOK: 978-0-9903989-1-2

Cover Illustration by Naomi Goldblatt-Bloom
Cover Design and Production by Rebecca Byrd Arthur

Printed in the United States of America

It is impossible to pretend that you are not heir to,
and therefore, however inadequately or unwillingly,
responsible to and for,
the time and place that give you life.

—James Baldwin

Acknowledgements

The story you are about to read is true. Some of the names have been changed to protect the innocent.

A portion of this book was previously published in the Alamo Bay Writers' Workshop Anthology, 2014, edited by Lowell Mick White.

I am truly grateful to Dr. Hazel Ward, Mrs. Marjorie Cooper Green and Robert "Bob" Smith who inspired me to write, T. C. Boyle, who encouraged me, and Pamela Booton who made it happen.

I want to thank Oreatha Easley, Colton Range, Kasey Guerrero, Darius Smith, all of whom are former students at ACC, and Jeremy Mitchell, my son. They read through pages upon pages of unedited manuscript and offered suggestions.

Deep gratitude goes to Diane Wilson whose question came right on time.

To Dr. Maya Angelou: you opened the gate and led the way.

Thanks to Jennifer Rangubphai, my executive assistant and Rahelina Razanadrafara for working the magic only the two of you can do.

Finally, I need to honor the memory of my mother, Mrs. Beulah Sherrod Williams; my aunts, Mrs. Minnie Bell Sherrod Parker, Mrs. Aileen Sherrod Davis, Mrs. Doretta Sherrod Davis and Mrs. Flora Sherrod Simms, all women for whom life was never a crystal stair.

A very special thanks to Sony/ATV Music Publishing for allowing me to use a portion of the song, "There's a Winner in You," written by Nickolas Ashford and Valerie Simpson. Copyright 1986 Nick O Val Music Co Inc. All rights on behalf of Nick O Val Music Co Inc. administered by Sony/ATV Music Publishing LLC, 8 Music Square West, Nashville, TN 37203. All rights reserved. Used by permission.

Preface

I dedicate this book to all alumni of Charles H. Darden High School. Everyone who ever attended Darden can identify with some of the stories I am about to tell. Though the school itself has gone through many transitions—a part of it burned, the part that remains is now an elementary school, the name has been assigned to a middle school—it is a powerful uniting force for several generations of former students. It is the class of 1962, however, my graduating class, that sparks my memory and brings us to this point in our history.

In May of 2010 we returned to the place of our origin to celebrate the forty-eighth anniversary of our high school graduation. Forty-eight years. I was excited, mostly because I had not seen so many of my classmates in all that time. We came from all over the country: North, South, East and West. We came loaded with childhood memories, pictures of children and grandchildren, stories of the past and stories of now. We came to giggle about secrets we used to hold, free ourselves of grudges we used to harbor, tell lies and truths about things that are and things that used to be. We came to honor those who had died. We wanted to know who had retired, who was still working or working again, who got fat, who got old. Most of us had already eaten the obligatory meal from Parker's Barbeque, and the funny thing about it is that fifty years ago we would have cherished an opportunity to sit down in that restaurant and enjoy a meal. Now, we (and some whites) still go to the back door. For comfort and fast service, maybe, or for just plain old times' sake. The food is cooked just inches away from the service counter and, pardon me, but I could not help but notice that some of the workers—the smiling, sweaty blacks—had been replaced by a group of grumpy, sweating whites, and for me, that made my lunch even more delicious.

I looked around the room at the *Meet and Greet* and I remembered how we were once called *colored,* and the truth is, I actually saw colors in that room. Some were glowing like sunshine, so I dubbed them yellow. Some were feisty, so I called them red. The lavender people had a cool, calm manner about them. There were those who were a smooth, Hershey chocolate, and those who were creamy vanilla. Of course there remained the haters; I colored them green. The shy ones who had blossomed into vibrant personalities were orange. Those with a majestic air were colored purple. We laughed and cried, hugged and kissed, screamed and whispered, snapped, pointed and high-fived each other. We told stories of triumph and failure, of cotton picking, sharecropping, and working in green tobacco. We started a discussion about living in the vacuum that permeates Wilson and is the mentality of every small town. In the midst of all the excitement, Gloria Carter's husband died on the golf course. And that colored everybody blue.

I AM THREE YEARS OLD. I AM PRETTY. *I have long hair and I only want to wear three plaits and a bang. Mary Joyce likes to put my hair into a whole lot of little plaits like the kids with nappy hair. But I don't want anybody to see me look ugly like that, so I fight with her. I scream until Mama takes the comb and brush and does my hair herself.*

Mama thinks I am pretty, too. She never tells me that, but I hear her tell Miss Louise. "She looks just like her daddy," she says. Mama is always bragging about how smart I am. She teaches me to speak proper English. I can count to one hundred in French. We go everywhere together, especially to the Ritz Theater on Friday nights when Daddy is at his poker game.

Today I am all dressed up. I have taken a bath in Sweetheart soap and it isn't even Sunday. I don't know where we're going, but it must be some place special. I have white ribbons in my hair. I wear my navy blue pleated skirt, my white blouse with the rounded collar, my navy blue sweater, my patent leather Sunday shoes and my white lace socks.

Mama holds my hand as we walk. I skip. I am happy. I am lucky, too, because I have my mama all to myself. James Earl has to share his mama with three other kids. He is my best friend.

Mama walks real fast. We cross Carroll Street and walk down. Pretty soon we pass Green Street. Then Viola. Then Vance and Faison. I can see the Center on Reid Street and I tug at Mama's skirt. I want to go play on the swings. "Not today," she says, and we keep walking. When we reach Academy Street we stop. Mama brushes my hair back with her hand. She makes me spit out my bubble gum. St. Alphonsus Catholic Church is on the left. We head towards the building on the right.

When we get there, Mama talks with a lady that smells good. I have seen her before. I saw her walking one day, I don't remember when, but I remember that her long dress flapped in the wind and made her look like a big, black crow.

I don't know why, but Mama leaves me with this lady. She takes me into a room where a lot of other kids are. I do not know any of them. They are bigger and older than I am. I turn to run back to my mother, but she is gone. The big crow lady grabs my shoulder and guides me to a chair. "This is your desk," she says. I start to cry. I do not know what anyone else is doing, but I am crying hard. Nobody asks me what's the matter. I can't believe my mama would leave me here. What did I do? Is this some kind of punishment? Maybe she found out about the eggs I put in my mud pies. I feel lost. I am so hurt. I feel like Mama does not love me anymore, so she gives me away to the black crow. I cry until I go to sleep.

Much later, Mama comes back to get me. She and the crow talk a little while. Mama holds me by the wrist. I can hear her voice as we walk home. I do not understand her words, but I know I am in trouble.

PART I
BONDAGE

One

I was raised in dirt road, out house, stewed chicken feet poverty—poverty so intense that it developed its own personality, its own odor. It had a way, this poverty, of camouflaging itself and making us believe that things were the way they were supposed to be. Most of my classmates and I did not realize how poor we were until we grew up and started to progress (or not). Some of us stayed forever, but a lot of us left, *escaped,* you might say. Either way, we came to recognize that we had grown up in a bubble that feigned a protection from the real world.

Wilson, North Carolina was a small, dusty, tobacco town with a railroad track that divided it into *colored* and white neighborhoods. Colored and white schools. Colored and white businesses. Colored and white toilets at the bus station, train station, and court house. We knew little about the white side of town except that you had to go there to buy groceries or pay the light bill or shop for clothes and shoes. And regardless of your heritage, if it was non-white, you lived and went to school in the colored section of Wilson.

Of course, our parents had access to the white settlement because many of our mothers worked in service; our fathers were yard boys. For many years my own mother worked at Jimmy Dempsey Laundry, sorting the dirty clothes of people who naturally assumed that black people were supposed to clean up after them and handle their filth. Because they did not know better, some of our parents simply submitted to this new kind of slavery. They had families to feed, and they had not yet entertained the notion that it is better to live freely as a pauper than to wallow in the lap of oppressed luxury. They considered it luxury to work for "good" white folks, to take home leftover ham and cake with which they could feed their own families, and to accept with beaming pride the outgrown shoes and clothes. These they would polish, or starch and iron, and give to their kids for school or church, and if there were items they could not use, they hand-delivered the pieces to someone less fortunate than they in our neighborhood. This was done with an air of benevolence and the absolute expectation that the favor would be returned.

The houses on our street were all the same. Some people called them *shotgun* houses; we called them *inways*. I suppose it was because if you went in one way and walked straight through you'd come out the other way. There was a front room, a middle room, and a kitchen. The spigot was on the back porch, and the outhouse was a few feet away in the back yard. Nearly every family had a grandmother who lived with them, and it was the grandmother who tended the gardens and kept the yard clean. She made yard brooms out of small tree branches, which she tied together with hemp. She took great pride in sweeping the front yard every Saturday morning. The broom made intricate little designs in the yard and nobody in our neighborhood—*nobody*—dared to disturb that pattern without permission. Since there were no telephones, visitors would just stop by, but they would stand at the edge of the yard and holler, "*Hoo…wooo.*" If one wanted company, she'd open the door, wave her arm and say, "Y'all come on in!" If she was busy, tired or sick, she simply did not respond to the holler, and the visitor would continue down the street.

Because there was no *living room,* the front room was kept ready for company with the chenille bedspread that the lady of the house purchased from the traveling salesman. He kept in the trunk of his car everything a household needed—dishes, glasses, pots and pans—and especially those pink and white rose-designed chenille bedspreads. They cost thirty dollars and he had an installment plan: fifty cents a week or two dollars a month, whichever was more convenient. He and Mr. Vick, the insurance man, were the only ones with gall enough to walk on the newly swept yard, and even they were met at the door with a scowl.

Electricity was a luxury. Many of our houses used candles or oil lamps for light. Winters were sometimes brutal in Wilson, so we filled pot-bellied stoves with kindling and half a bucket of coal. A splash of kerosene and a lighted stick match provided heat throughout the entire house if we kept all the doors open.

Nothing was wasted in those days. Women often inverted soda bottles into the ground to line the walkway to the house. Boys bent the bottle cap over the tip of a stick and used it as an arrow for fishing or hunting rabbits. Aunt Doretta cut old tires into triangles on one side, painted them white, and used them as yard pots for geraniums. Mama tore brown paper bags into strips and twisted them to make hair curlers. Grandma took worn out socks that could not stand yet another darning and used them as dust rags. She saved buttons and zippers from shirts, pants, dresses and Army uniforms. And each piece that looked like it had no more life in it was cut into squares or rectangles and sewn together to make a quilt. Leftover bread and biscuits were mixed with sugar, eggs, milk and raisins to make bread pudding. The grease from ham and bacon seasoned collard greens and black-eyed peas. Almost everyone had a small garden, and each year they would *put up* tomatoes, beets, peaches and pickled watermelon rinds. I believe my people invented *recycling.*

So this is the way we survived in the days before welfare and food stamps. Not that my parents would have taken such charity--they were both such proud people. My father was illiterate, but he was pretty—pretty as a girl, almost. He was tall and light-skinned, with wavy hair and a kingly attitude. He was trained in dry wall plastering, and he was good at it. When it rained, and it rained a lot in Wilson, he could not work. So he didn't, because some things were beneath him. Don't get me wrong; he was a hustler. He used to cook at the Do Drop Inn, and the Silver Boot, and the Snooty Fox. He'd come home in the middle of the night and wake us up with a platter of fried chicken and fluffy biscuits, and then we'd all go back to sleep, our bellies full, and our minds content that all was right with the world.

But something broke him. And while I would be a grown woman before I could put it all together, I remember the exact moment it happened.

I AM FOUR YEARS OLD. I HAVE A NEW LITTLE BROTHER. *He is different from the last one. The last one was white. I could see through his skin. He did not stay long. One day Dr. Barnes said he was dead. So they took him away. His name was Cornell. This one is dark. They name him Wiley, Jr. I don't think they like him. I hear Grandma Easter say, "He's a fine boy. He just black." Then Daddy gets mad and he beats up my Mama. I scream and beg him to stop. Grandma Easter smiles and walks away.*

Today is Friday. Daddy comes home early from his poker game. He hollers at Mama and makes her take me and Jr. to Mrs. Wilson's house. Mama is crying when she leaves us. Me too. I peep out the window. I see Daddy slap her and make her get into the car. They are gone all night. When she comes to get us in the morning, Mama is still crying. Her face is swollen. It looks like she fell down on it. She tells us to be quiet because Daddy is asleep.

Now it is Saturday night. Daddy is leaving for his game. He stands at the front door and hollers at Mama again. He says he will kill her if she leaves the house. All the neighbors hear him say this. When Daddy leaves, Miss Louise comes to our house. She says, "What happened?" Mama puts Jr. in his crib. She blows her nose and puts me in the corner to color. "Stay in the lines," she tells me.

I like to color. I mix blue and red to make purple. Orange and green make brown. I sing in French: "Allons enfants de la patrié. Le jour de gloire est arrivé!" Mama and Miss Louise speak softly, but I hear every word:

"He came home yesterday mad as hell. Somebody told him something. He wanted to take the baby to a doctor for a blood test. I told him, 'Wiley, you can't believe everything you hear in them streets. You know people are always trying to make trouble for other people.' He denied being Jr.'s daddy, just like he denied Barbr'ann. God fixed it so she come here looking just like him. But Jr. is dark. He said, 'Ain't no way a yella man and a yella woman can have a black baby.' He don't stop to think. My daddy was black. His own daddy is black. He just don't stop to think about that."

I stop singing. Mama and Miss Louise look at me. I want to correct Mama's English the way she does me, but I am not supposed to be listening. Besides, I know what she will say: "Don't do as I do; do as I say do." I pretend to be busy choosing a crayon. I hear Mama say,

"So I told him, 'If you gonna take the baby to the doctor, I'm going, too.' I know him, see. He'd come back here, tell me anything and kill me for nothing. So when I said that, he put the baby down, told me to go get in the car. He made me take the younguns over to old lady Wilson's house, and then he took me to the woods, out by the lake. It was dark out there. I was scared. But as God is my witness, my conscience is clear. And I trusted the Lord to save me. He took a piece of rope from the back seat and tied me to a tree. He opened the trunk and took out his shotgun. I watched him load it, praying all the time. But I didn't say a word to him. He sat on the back of the car and pointed that gun at my face all night. He pitched and reared… accused me of all kinds of things. He was a crazy man--crazy! He kept saying, 'Why you do this to me?' Every time I try to defend myself he'd tell me to shut up. I cried. I couldn't help it. I really thought he was going to kill me. I peed on myself. I started praying. I promised God that if He would get me out of this alive, I'd stay and take care of Wiley for the rest of my life. Way after while he untied me and put the gun away.

"I don't know what I'm going to do. I didn't do nothing." *She blows her nose again. She says,* "I always loved that nigger much too much, but now… I'm scared of him. I don't want to stay here. But I promised God!" *Then she*

14

starts to cry really hard. Miss Louise hugs her. "Lord have mercy," *she says.*

After that, everything changed. Every time my little brother cried, or ate, or pooped his diaper, Daddy would holler at Mama. Sometimes he wouldn't go to work. He spent a lot of his time in bed with a legal pad and a pencil, which he used to write down numbers, *myriads* of them. On Friday nights he would bathe, get dressed in his grey suit and the new shirt that Mama had just bought, tuck two cigars into his jacket pocket, carefully arrange his Stetson by tilting it just slightly to the left and go off until early Saturday morning. Sometimes he'd come home with a wad of money and make Mama beg for some of it. Other times he'd come home without his watch, or his ring, with nothing but lint in his pockets.

He was such a braggart, Daddy was. I remember once we all went to visit Grandpa Starkey who lived in the country near Sharpsburg. After he and Grandma Easter separated Grandpa Starkey married a woman named Annie who was much younger than he. They had a whole lot of children. Charlie was the oldest and he was two years younger than I. It was hog killing time and Daddy and Grandpa cooked a pig in a hole in the ground. Mama and Aunt Annie made cabbage and boiled potatoes and chocolate cake and homemade ice cream. I called her Aunt Annie because she was younger than my mama. Besides, I already had two grandmas.

Daddy had left Grandpa's house when he was only twelve years old and he had fended for himself ever since. I suppose he wanted his father to think that he had made the right choice when he said, "Yeah. I'm doing real good in Wilson. Got my own car, a good job. Got money in the bank."

Then Grandpa said, "Well, Son. Look like you would give Daddy something." And Daddy clenched his mouth shut tight as a coffin.

We used to be good friends, Daddy and I. He took me with him on long walks. All his friends called me "Little Wiley." And then one day, when I was four, he took me to Mrs. Brodie's house when Mr. Brodie was out of town. He bought me an ice cream sandwich from the truck and left me on the porch swing to eat it while he went inside. When we got home, I told Mama about my day. Daddy stopped taking me with him after that.

two

Grandma Easter ran a brothel. Of course, that's an educated word I had no way of knowing at the time. But it was at her house that I had my first exposure to sex. The house was on Wiggins Street. It sat on tall sticks and I used to play in the dirt under it. I could hear the grownups laughing, drinking and dancing. Sometimes they'd cuss. Sometimes people would fight. The men gave money to Grandma Easter. She always wore an apron, and she was almost always frying fish.

She had a boyfriend named Mr. Dave. He was tall and black, black. He worked at the Quarry. He'd come home from work with rock dust all over him. Grandma always had his supper ready.

My daddy was her youngest child and her favorite. He looked like her. She was short, and she had some meat on her bones. She had big, fat, pretty legs and she talked very loud. She loved me. And when she wanted me to take a nap she'd give me a little shot of bourbon and some Coca-Cola. She tried to teach me how to dip snuff, but I couldn't stand the taste of it. I visited with her often. One day, she was mad about something and she started cussing and throwing things. There were a lot of rooms in her house. She raised her foot and kicked open the door to every one of them. I was standing at her side when she kicked open one door, and I saw a man and woman naked on the bed. I didn't understand what they were doing, and I really didn't understand the words Grandma used: "I want all you mother fuckers out of my house right now." The man and woman both looked at me. They were really, really scared. She sent me outside, and just as I was leaving I heard somebody say she was a hell raiser. She went into her room and came back with a gun. People scattered like roaches. A little later she set the table and called me in to eat. She filled her bottom lip with snuff and waited for Mr. Dave to come home.

* * *

We moved a lot when I was little. Sometimes we'd stay with Aunt Dolly Mae or Aunt Minnie Bell. Sometimes we had our own house. All the streets in our neighborhood were unpaved: Darden Alley, Queen Street, Viola Street, Vance Street. But Green Street was paved, and that's where my mother wanted to live. That was the street where the teachers lived. The one *colored* doctor, the one *colored* dentist, the one *colored* professor, all lived on that street. It was beautiful and tree-lined with a sidewalk, and everybody who was anybody lived there. My great-uncle, C. E. Artis, had a huge white house on Green Street that was also his mortuary. But by this time, Daddy had stopped working. A man came to the door one day and asked to speak to Wiley Williams. I was standing right by Mama when I heard her tell the man, "He's not here." "Yes, he is, Mama!" I said, and I went running through the house calling him. "Daddy! Daddy! Somebody's here to see you!" My father was hiding in a closet. He grabbed me and covered my mouth. When the man left, my daddy yelled at me, "Don't you ever do that again!" The next day Mama got a job at Dempsey Laundry.

That's about the time that my childhood ended. My mother and I used to go to the Ritz Theater on Friday nights while Daddy was out, and she would buy me a hot dog and popcorn and a Coca Cola. Most of the time I would fall asleep during the movie (except for *Gone With the Wind,* I stayed awake for the whole show), and then we'd walk back home. On Saturdays we'd clean the house and listen to Sepia Serenade on the radio. Then we'd go uptown and shop, pay bills, buy groceries. She would get something for me every time—cotton candy, hair ribbons, a pair of patent leather shoes for church. But all of that came to an end when Mama went to work.

I was six years old. Mama walked the two miles to the laundry because we no longer had a car. She'd leave home at 5:30 in the morning, so it became my job to empty the slop jar and take my little brother to Grandma Josephine's house before I went to school.

Mrs. Josephine Artis Sherrod was Mama's mama. Some people say she was a saint. I think it is because she raised so many children. She had twelve of her own, and in the middle of them, the "old man," as she called Grandpa, got a child with another woman. Grandma took Uncle Booker T. in and raised him as her own. She also raised my cousin, Eloise. She was Uncle Elmer's daughter. They all lived together in Uncle Shird's house. He was my rich uncle. A plumber by trade, he only had a third grade education. But he had a gift of building houses, and he built or bought every house in his block on Viola Street. He also built a store, which is why Mama named the 800 block of Viola St. *Sherrod Village.*

I don't remember much about Grandpa Sherrod; I just know that he was still mad at Mama when he died. She told me that she said something one time that hurt his feelings: "You didn't do so good when you got Booker T." Years later I would figure out that their argument was about me.

Taking out the slop jar was a chore that I hated, so I would post-pone it until just before Mama came home from work at 6:30 in the evening. We always had a peach tree in our yard. Once in a while Mama would come home early, and if I had not done my chores properly, my mother would sting my legs with a peach tree switch.

One would think that with an added income things would get better, but it seems to me now that we stopped progressing when Mama went to work. My brother and I were hungry all the time. We used to steal plums and pecans from the Satchells' backyard, and I would cook whatever I could find. We'd go down the street to Grandma Josephine's house in hopes that she'd offer us something to eat. It would have been okay to take it because she was a relative. Once in a while Grandma would cut an orange into four pieces. She'd give a piece to me, one to Jr., one to Eloise and keep a piece for herself. Jr. and I would quickly eat ours. Eloise would always save hers until later when we were hungry again. For her it was a treat. For us it was a meal. I will never forget the smug look on her face when she said, "No. You had yours."

When I was seven years old, I got a job at Sally Shackleford's neighbor-hood grocery store and that helped us a lot. I made fifty cents a week, but it was enough to take Jr. and me to Drake Theater where we could feast on hot dogs and popcorn, and stay all day.

Then Daddy left us and went to Washington D. C. and everything changed for the worse. My mother was sad all the time. Tired *all the time.* And angry. She'd work all day long and then come home and go to bed. If anything went wrong in that house, she found a way to make it my fault. Sometimes I felt like she blamed me for being born.

She used to sing. Now she just talked, talked, talked. In every word there was a complaint. About three times a week she'd say, "Bring me a switch."

I did not know it then, but for the next ten years my father would be a *sometime* parent. About once a month he'd wire my mother twenty dollars. Two or three times a year he'd come home for a weekend to check up on us, but he never brought any money. I started cooking for the entire family four days before my seventh birthday. It was supposed to be a surprise for Mama when she turned twenty-five, but it became a permanent assign-ment. Cooking was just another added chore on top of the cleaning and ironing and taking care of my brother. I started to feel like I was Mama's wife because if I didn't have all my work done when she came home, I'd get a whipping.

three

Uncle Jarvis worked at Carolina General Hospital. I never knew what he did there, but he wore a dark green uniform all the time. He always had on heavy brown boots, and his pocket watch dangled from his belt along with a bunch of skeleton keys. During the depression after World War II, when even people who had money had to use food vouchers because of the rations, Uncle Jarvis would bring Mama horse meat that he had taken from the hospital. He also brought potatoes, powdered milk, eggs and cheese. He would come to our house to deliver these goods and then he'd ask Mama to write a letter for him to his wife, Aunt Susanna. Mama eagerly grabbed her ink, filled her Schaeffer pen, and waited for Uncle Jarvis to dictate. She took great pride in the fact that she had received more education than any of her siblings, and she was the scribe for all of them.

I noticed that Uncle Jarvis had started wearing his shirt on the outside. Naturally, I was curious about it, so I asked him.

"Well, I declare, Barbr'ann. You don't miss a thang do ya?"

"No sir."

"Okay, well, I have this thing the doctors call a rupture. So I wear my shirt on the outside to hide it."

"A rupture? What's that?"

"It's like a swelling in my private part."

"Oh." I tried to keep my eyes on his face even though I wanted to look right at that area. "Does it hurt?"

"Little bit. 'Specially when I walk. *Specially* when I ride my bicycle."

Since the bicycle was the primary means of transportation for the men in our community, I could see how that could get in the way of all Uncle Jarvis' business—going to work, going to church, going to see Aunt Susanna.

"Can the doctor fix it?"

"Well…they gon' try. I'm gonna have a operation next week."

"But what if—"

"Barbr'ann!" My mother interrupted, "Stay in your little girl place and stop asking so many questions."

I loved Uncle Jarvis. He had taught me how to play horseshoes and shoot marbles. I wanted to know as much as I could about his rupture and his operation. In spite of Mama I found myself following him around and eavesdropping on his conversations. Then one day, he and Grandma Josephine and I were sitting on the front porch admiring a huge catfish that Uncle Jarvis had just caught. The operation was scheduled for the next day. The doctors at Carolina General had promised to do it for free because they liked him so much. I heard him tell Grandma, "Mama, I feel like this is the last time I'm gon' see y'all."

Grandma said, "Son, if you feel that way, just don't go."

Uncle Jarvis said, "I have to. It's reached the point where I can't even stand up straight. My balls are halfway down my thighs."

I got up and went to the swing. That way I could look at them without them knowing that I was listening. Uncle Jarvis gave Grandma some money and told her what to do with it. He told her what he wanted to wear at his funeral in case he died. And he told her that he had bought a plot from Uncle Shird. He stood up and hugged Grandma, and that was the only time in my life that I ever saw her shed a tear. She promised to pray for him and, as he was leaving, he said to me: "Barbr'ann, you take good care of my mama, ya hear?"

The next day Uncle Jarvis died on the operating table. The doctor said he had a heart attack during surgery and there was nothing they could do to save him.

In those days, when the undertaker had finished his job, he released the body to the family. He placed a wreath—usually black for men, white for women—on the front door. The casket was open all day and night as it rested in the parlor of the house, and people would come in to pay their respects and sign the register. They brought cooked food and money, and I had never seen or heard so much quiet. Everyone whispered as they offered their sympathy.

I stayed at Grandma's house for the entire two-day long wake. I remember kissing Uncle Jarvis on his forehead. His skin was hard and cold. I started to cry because I realized that once they put him in the ground at Rest Haven, I would never see him again.

I was still crying when we got the news that Grandma Easter was at Mercy Hospital. Mr. Dave came home early from work that day and he beat her really bad when he found all those people in his house. She was unconscious.

My daddy left us and went running to the hospital. When he came back he said that Grandma was in a coma. The next day, Mama went with Daddy.

When they returned, Mama told me that Grandma was asking for Aunt Tine.

My mother was not Grandma Easter's favorite daughter-in-law; it was Aunt Tine whom she favored. But it was my mother who went to see her in the hospital. Grandma would call out for Aunt Tine and Daddy made Mama answer her. Grandma stayed like that for two weeks, never awakening, but constantly calling: "Tine…Tine…"

At the beginning of the third week, Grandma Easter died. At her funeral Daddy tried to fight Mr. Dave. The pall bearers pulled them apart while my daddy kept screaming, "I'll kill you! I'll kill you! What did she ever do to you?!"

I was still grieving the death of Uncle Jarvis. Now, two of my favorite people were dead. I cried for days. I cried so much, I got sick. When I wasn't crying I was sleeping. I couldn't eat anything. I was burning up with fever, and my head hurt so bad I could hardly move my eyes. Dr. Barnes came to the house and told Mama he couldn't do anything for me. "She's grieving." he said, "and she will have to fight her way through this." Mama sent for Mrs. Mattie Mercer.

"Ma Matt" we called her. She was a self-appointed healer, of sorts, who lived in our neighborhood on the corner of Queen and Reid Streets. She was the one who told Mama that Cornell had pneumonia. She was the one who prayed over Jr. when he reached two years old and still couldn't walk. She was the one who "fixed" women when they got a baby they did not want. And now she came to see me.

Ma Matt told Mama to chip some ice and put it in a basin with a little water. She bathed me all over. The cold water made me shiver. She cut an onion in half and held it to the bottoms of my feet. She worked on me for a long time. The onions turned brown, and after a while, I started to sweat. She cut three oranges and squeezed the juice into my mouth. She asked me how I felt and I told her I felt good. I did.

I AM NINE YEARS OLD. MY COUSIN LIVES IN OUR HOUSE. *He is eighteen. And big. I am alone in the house with him a lot. I don't remember when it started. I must have been about seven or eight, I guess, because by nine I am experienced enough to know that it is wrong. I don't like what we do. I feel ashamed. He does nasty to me. The only reason I know it is wrong is that I have never seen Mama do it. It is a secret that only nasty people do, like the man and woman at Grandma Easter's house. Cousin touches me in places that*

21

only Mama has seen. He tells me not to tell. He says he will kill me if I do. I am afraid. I stay quiet because even if I do tell Mama and she does something to him, she is at work all day long. He could kill me while she is gone. Besides, he doesn't hurt me. He makes me feel special. He touches me on the tickle part between my legs. He rubs it with his thumb while he pulls his thing back and forth until it throws up. Sometimes he kisses me there. I like that part. It feels good. I welcome it. I even ask for it. I would let him do that every day except my thighs get sore because of his whiskers.

My brother catches us doing nasty. He says he will tell Mama. Cousin says he will kill him, too. So we keep quiet. But Jr. holds it over my head. He blames me. He says he will tell Mama anyway if I don't fix him something to eat.

We go to Grandma Josephine's house and stay for a long time. Jr. is ready to go. I am not. I want to wait until she feeds us. Jr. says she won't give us anything. We argue about whether to go or stay. He says, "I'ma tell Mama." So we leave.

After a while I decide to tell Mama myself. It is Saturday morning. Mama is wearing her blue bathrobe. We stand in the kitchen. Jr. waits in a corner. His arms are folded. His eyes look at me, then Mama, then me again. I tell Mama how Cousin does nasty to me. I give her every detail. She says, "Why didn't you tell me before?" I say, "'Cause he said he will kill me, Mama!" I throw myself on her and hug her waist. She says, "Well don't ever let your daddy find out." She does not hug me back, so I feel like it is my fault. I can never let my daddy know how bad I have been.

After that Cousin does nasty to the girl next door. He calls her Sugar Plum. She is twelve. She acts like she likes it. Cousin sends me outside. He gives me a whistle and tells me to blow it if anyone comes. They do it every day. Nobody ever comes. Sugar Plum gets big. Her mother makes them get married. Then both of them live in our house.

four

I am often amazed at the strength of my memory. The power of my imagination. I remember a day when I fell out of a tree and tore my leg open on a broken branch. As Mama bandaged my wound she said, "I can't wait until you get twelve. Then you won't be a little girl anymore. Maybe you will cut out some of your tom-boyish ways." I never asked her what she meant; I figured it out on my own. I convinced myself that I would turn into a boy at twelve. Nothing and no one could tell me anything different. Not even Mary Joyce.

Mary Joyce was one of Aunt Dolly Mae's daughters. She was about three years older than I and very sophisticated. She knew almost everything, and I trusted her. Well, at least I trusted her until the day she told me the *truth* about boys and girls. She used words like *screwin'* and *menastratin'*, when I was ten, but I didn't believe her. I had already caught her in a lie about Santa Claus. So, when she described those words I put my fist in my mouth. And when she told me where babies come from, how *I*, in fact, got here, I thought I would eat my whole hand. "Boys don't *menastrate*," she said. "But everybody screws. Your mama screws." I knew that was a lie, too, because my mama wouldn't ever do anything like that.

I developed an elaborate plan to punish the boys in my play group for the mean things they had done to me. Happy, Puddin' and Solo were Aunt Minnie Bell's sons. Their nick-names were very fitting. Happy was always smiling. Puddin' was sweet and easy-going. Solo never did run with the herd. In fact, it was Solo who saved my life one day. Happy used to lock me in a dark closet every time we played hide and seek. To this day I can't figure out why I chose to hide in that same closet. On this particular day we were playing cowboys and Indians, and, being the only girl, I was chosen to be the Indian. They captured me and tied me to a tree. They let Clarence Barnes kiss me all over my face. Bosie, the dog, humped my leg. I was *not* a sissy, but when they put a bunch of dried leaves and twigs around my feet, and Happy pulled a stick match and a rock out of his pocket, I began to cry. Solo ran to get Aunt Minnie Bell just before Happy struck that match.

So I would get them back when I turned into a boy. It just made sense that they would turn into girls. My plan was to leave Solo alone because I saw him as a protector. Not that I needed a whole lot of protection—I could do everything they could do, one on one, and better. I could make bows and arrows, shoot marbles, and pee standing up. But I could not fight them all at one time. I would get them and get them good. They, however, would have to wait. Mary Joyce was stupid, and she was mean. I would get her first for lying about my mama.

As it turned out, Mary Joyce was right.

I AM TWELVE YEARS OLD. I AM IN THE EIGHTH GRADE. *We study the reproductive system. I learn the truth about how babies are made. I am mad at my mother. She has not warned me about this, and I feel like a fool. It is a big and disastrous surprise. The girls in Health class laugh at me because I did not know. I want to run and cry, but I am determined to learn all I can about this.*

Within the week I start my own period. It happens while I am asleep. My cousin comes home and turns on the light. He wakes up Mama and she comes to help me. "Don't be scared," she says. But I am not scared; I already know about it. I'm just mad, mad, mad!

Mama heats some water and bathes me. She goes into the closet and gets a sanitary belt and a Kotex. She shows me how to put them on. She says, "Change them three or four times a day. Do not flush them down the toilet. Wrap them up in newspaper and take them outside to the garbage can." Then she tells me about the time she started her period. She says that she was working in green tobacco when it happened. She kept going to the outhouse and wiping herself with newspaper. She didn't know how she could explain to her mother how she could hurt herself down there.

I look at her real funny. She has kept this secret from me the way her mother kept it from her. What else is she hiding? I don't think I can ever trust her again.

My mother kept a close eye on me and the calendar after that. Every month she'd ask me if I started. If I said yes, I'd have to prove it. Three months after my periods started, they stopped. Just stopped coming altogether. Mama and Daddy argued for weeks about how I got *big*. Daddy blamed her for not watching me. She defended herself by saying she had to work. They fought a lot, and I tried to tell them that I had not done anything. But I was gaining weight. I had made a red circular skirt in Mrs. Jenkins' class. It took me three months to make that skirt. By the time I finished it, it was too small at the waist. Mama watched me as I tried it on, and when the button wouldn't close I said, "Guess I'm getting fat." She went into a frenzy. "Lord have mercy! Lord have mer-ceeeee!" She lectured me and prayed; she prayed and lectured: "Looks like you're gonna have a baby. I am only thirty years old. Too young to be a grandmother."

I knew how babies were made and I knew I had not done that. I reasoned that God had done it, the way He did for Mary. I went to see James Earl and I actually proposed to him. I told him that God have given me a baby that would save the world. Maybe it would be a girl this time. I told him that an angel would come to him and explain the whole thing. When James Earl didn't seem as enthusiastic about it as I was, I went to his brother, Preston. Then to a boy across the street, Joe Moore. None of them was interested at all in being somebody's earthly father.

Then one Saturday morning I saw Mr. Fitch, the mailman, coming down the street. I ran to get the mail. My father snatched the mail out of my hands and, as it turned out, there was a letter for me from a boy I had met in the movies the previous weekend. Now they had a suspect. My eagerness to get the mail had proven my guilt. I must have known the letter was coming.

Mama read the letter out loud:

> *Dear Barbara,*
> *When I saw you last week I thought you were the prettiest girl*
> *have ever seen. I loved the way you pulled the hair on my arm.*
> *I hope you can meet me on Sunday at one o'clock. Maybe you*
> *can leave your little brother at home. See you then?*
> *Love,*
> *Tommy*

There was no return address on the envelope but Daddy was furious. He hollered at me and he hollered at Mama. He said he would find that boy and make him marry me. I didn't want to get married. I didn't really like that boy. In fact, I had forgotten all about him until the letter came. But there was no denying . Daddy said, "Your Mama's a fast woman, and you just like her." And that ended all talk on the subject.

Mama sent me to borrow a cup of sugar from Aunt Minnie Bell. It wasn't long before I realized that the real reason I was there was so that

Aunt Minnie Bell could talk to me. Or, rather, that I would talk to her. It was no secret that we were close friends, especially after she rescued me from Happy. She asked me questions about what I had done. I tried to defend myself again, but after a while I started to cry. "You must tell your mama who the boy is," she said. But when I couldn't come up with a name, she let me go. She said she didn't have any sugar, so she sent me to the store to get some. When I got back home, Mama and Aunt Minnie Bell were talking about me. Each of them stopped abruptly and stared at me. Finally, Aunt Minnie Bell said, "Barbr'ann, you say you didn't do anything, but that's a secret that will not keep. Beulah, you better take her to the doctor." Mama said, "She's just like her damn daddy; tell a lie in a minute."

With that I was hauled off to Dr. Cowan's office for the most humiliating experience of my life. He put me on a table and lifted my skirt, right in front of Mama. He rubbed my belly and put his finger inside me. At last he said to Mama, "There's nothing in there. Her hymen is intact." Mama said, "But I don't understand. She hasn't had a period in months." Then Dr. Cowan said, "Well, maybe she's anemic. He prescribed Unicap Vitamins and told me to take one a day. After about three weeks, my period started again.

Nobody apologized for calling me names. Nobody congratulated me for telling the truth. Our life continued as it was before, but I was relieved that I did not have to get married and be somebody's mother.

IAM THIRTEEN AND IN THE NINTH GRADE at Charles H. Darden High School. I live on Viola Street next to Mr. and Mrs. Satchell. Mr. Satchell teaches music at our school. He is the one who wrote our Alma Mater. Mrs. Satchell teaches math at Speight High School out in the country. They have no children. I think Mrs. Satchell knows that Jr. and I steal her plums, even though she never says anything to us about it, and she never complains to Mama. Mrs. Satchell advises the Marian Anderson Civic Club, an organization that chooses the best "colored" teenage girls and teaches them how to be ladies. Though she calls me "Dah-ling," and Sugaaaarrr," she does not invite me to join that club. Instead, she comes over every day to find out what I learned in Algebra class. She takes notes, and she praises me for my thoroughness. Then she teaches her class our lessons the next day.

Mr. Branford is my home-room teacher. My house is less than a block away from the school, but I am late every day. Mama wakes me up at 5:30 in the morning before she goes to work. She tells me to do my chores before going to school. I promise. As soon as she leaves, I go back to bed. The bell rings at 8:15. I am never there before 8:20. So, when Mr. Branford growls and looks at me real funny, I apologize, but I don't think anything of it. He looks around the classroom and then, back at me. He says, "Barb'ann, after school today I want you to go to Mr. Brown's room."

I panic. Mr. Ellis Brown is in charge of detention. If I go to detention, Mama will get home before I do. I have not washed the dishes. I have not taken out the slop jar. That's a good whipping right there. I start to make up believable excuses to tell Mr. Brown when Mr. Branford says, "The captain of the Patrol Force wants to see you."

Now I am excited. The Patrol Force monitors the halls when we change classes. They wear silver badges. They collect money at the football andbasketball games. They sponsor socials and serve as ushers at school events. I hope this means that I will join the force.

I have a permit to leave campus at lunch time. A plate lunch costs twenty-five cents a day. We cannot afford that, so Mama signed a paper to let me go home for lunch. I don't understand that; there is nothing to eat at home. Most of the time I go to Grandma, Aunt Doretta, my cousin Sudie Mae or Uncle Shird and "borrow" enough money to eat lunch at school. A nickel here, a dime there, maybe three or four pennies. Sometimes I am successful; sometimes I am not. But the process is time-consuming. Normally, by the time I get back to school, the line is closing.

So, on this day I run home during lunch break and do my chores. Mama will be pleased at the idea of a late meeting at school. She likes to have me in things. I am already in the Glee Club, and I sing in the Junior Choir at church.

The bell rings at 3:15 in the afternoon. I go to the girl's room first, in case it is a long meeting. I arrive a little late and take a seat in the back. There is a discussion on the floor about some upcoming event. Nobody seems to agree on anything. The captain stands quietly waiting for order. After a while he says, "We can all sing together, but everybody can't talk at one time." With that the noise grows louder. A girl stands and points her finger at someone by the window. Someone yells, "Sit down and shut up!" The captain repeats, "Everybody can't talk at one time!"

There is something about his voice that makes me pay attention. I focus on him as if no one else is there. He wears an oxford shirt, pullover sweater and well-creased slacks. His skin is the color of caramel. Not a mark on it. The afternoon sun shines through the blinds and makes it look like he has a halo. His eyes are large under raised brows, and he chews on the right corner of his bottom lip. For a moment he stands that way, immobile, studying the group of irate students. I stand up. I don't know what it is. I just want to put my hands on him. But I am paralyzed with fear, or something. I cannot define what I feel. I can't figure out what is wrong with me. I keep my eyes on him as if my breath depends on it. Nothing else matters. No one else lives. I can't even remember my name. I feel like I've been hoodoo'd or something. Mesmerized by the aura of him.

His voice, smooth as velvet, quick as lightning, brings me to my senses. He places a hand on his hip and says, "Da-amn!"

My knees buckle. I grab my desk and sit down. My heart is racing and I feel all butterfly in the pit of my stomach. I blink my eyes and shake my head, but it is no use. I am hopelessly in love.

Somehow he manages to get order. When the meeting is over the new officers have to sign the roster. Nearly everyone leaves and I am still glued to my seat, watching him. He looks at me and I have to catch my breath to keep from swallowing my tongue.

"Mr. Branford send you?"

I nod.

"Sure you want to be a part of this madness?"

I nod again.

"What's the matter? Cat got your tongue?"

How can I tell him that love has me hog-tied, tongue-tied? Words of love fill my throat and stick there in a painful lump like peanut butter. I place my hand over my mouth. What if I blabber something stupid and let him know I love him? This secret is mine, and I need the strength of God Almighty to get out of this chair. I shake my head "no."

He laughs a little. "Well, what's your name? Come on over here and sign your name."

"It's Barb…It's um…um…" I take a deep breath. "My name is Barbara."

Stumbling to my feet I straighten my skirt and walk towards him, the rolling thunder of heaven in my chest.

"Well, Barbara, I'm James…" He pushes the sign-up sheet towards me. "But my friends call me 'Pop.'"

I want to be his friend. What's more, with his teeth firmly fastened to his lip like that, I have the strangest urge to kiss him. I think it is his voice. Smooth as vanilla ice cream. Makes me want to lick the spoon.

But I am, after all, a child to him. And a subordinate. We talk briefly, or rather, he talks and I listen. I eat up every word like it is my last supper. Somehow, above the noise inside of me I understand that we have a lot in common.

We are both in the school choir, each of us wants to go to college, both our mothers are pregnant, and no, he does not have a girlfriend.

I am a few months away from my fourteenth birthday, which means I am a few months away from being able to take company. But I already know that one day, James Outlaw will be my boyfriend. I make sure everybody else knows it, too. Boys my own age don't interest me. I focus all my attention on Pop. I fantasize every single day about kissing him. I have never kissed a boy, but I have seen a lot of movies. The woman in the movie wraps her arm around the man's neck and stands tippy-toe on one foot. Looks like she folds into him. Since I am already taller than Pop, I don't think that part will work, but I am still willing to try it. First thing, though, I need some practice. I think about trying out my kisses on James Earl or Braxton or Maurice, but they probably don't know any more about it than I do. That first kiss holds so much promise, and I don't want to waste it on a novice.

I decide to practice alone. I stand in front of the mirror and pin my hair high off my neck. I open my blouse, tuck my collar under my bra straps and pull it off my shoulder. I look like Dorothy Dandridge. Leaning forward I purse my lips, close my eyes and plant a passionate kiss on the mirror. I feel absolutely nothing. I try again with my eyes open. Better, but not quite right. I squint my eyes almost shut and kiss the mirror again, moving my tongue from side to side. Perfect. I can see my image. I can smell my breath on the mirror.

Next, I practice the kick. This part is difficult. I can't get my arms around the mirror. So, I step over to the bed and hug the bedpost, kissing the top of the spindle. I spend most of the morning watching myself kiss myself and kissing and hugging the bedpost, drawing back my foot slower, slower, until I can do it with grace and ease. I don't know how I will get Pop to cooperate. Maybe I will say something like "Kiss me, you fool," the way the woman does in the movie. But the more I get to know him, the more convinced I am that he is the right choice.

five

My mother had been sick for a long time. She was pale and weak, and she had a growth in her stomach area, yet she still went to work every day. Her fear was evident and she did not try to hide it from me. It was the fall of 1958. Winters in North Carolina are sometimes brutal, and this one was particularly cold and wet. Snow, sleet and harsh winds met Mama almost every morning as she set out for her two mile trek to Jimmie Dempsey. She'd put on two pairs of socks and cover her head with a kerchief and a plastic scarf, fill a mayonnaise jar with coffee and give me instructions for the day before she left. Her eyes told a story of hopelessness. "I don't know how to reach your daddy," she'd say, "But if anything happens to me, make sure you take good care of your brother." Then she would rub her belly and squeeze my hand tightly.

Daddy came home that Christmas and he made Mama go to Dr. Sullivan. The result was more devastating than a tumor. Mama was pregnant. My father lost his mind. The fights turned into downright beatings. "Ain't no way in hell a man can be with a woman for ten years and nothing happens, then boom! All of a sudden she big." He screamed this at her from the front yard, on the back porch, at family gatherings. It was as if he had to have an audience, and the more people came out of their houses to listen, the louder and more violent he became.

One morning as Mama was washing breakfast dishes just before church, Daddy charged at her. She tried to run, but the kitchen was so small there was no place to go. He held her by the shoulder with one hand and he pounded her in the face with the other. He kept dipping his fist into the dish water, filled with bacon and egg remnants. I tried to get between them, crying and begging him to stop. But he said, "Get the hell out of here. I'm mad all over!" He broke her glasses, and he beat her until he was exhausted. When he went to get a towel to wipe his face, Mama ran out the back door to Aunt Minnie Bell's house.

At first, Daddy didn't seem to notice that Mama was gone. He ranted and raved throughout the house, breaking things and cussing at the air. I grabbed Jr. and crouched in a corner, watching him. I was scared. I bit my nails until my fingers bled. The tension in that house made me want to run away, but I had to protect my little brother.

After a while, Daddy asked me: "Where yo' mama?" I told him I didn't know. Just about that time, Aunt Minnie Bell came in the house. She and Daddy talked for a minute, but he did not raise his voice to her. She said, "Beulah scared of you. But damn if I'm scared. You wanna fight somebody, fight me!" Then Daddy said, "I would if my back wasn't hurting."

That was a defining moment for me. Aunt Minnie Bell was tough; she'd fight Uncle Thomas like a man. Daddy was afraid of her, and I realized right then that the only reason he beat up on Mama was because he could. I never quite saw him the same after that, and I vowed that as soon as I was grown I'd get away from Wilson, away from him and away from everybody like him.

Through all of this he never once told us that his girlfriend was pregnant, too.

I AM FOURTEEN YEARS OLD. FINALLY. *My sister was born two months early, on April Fool's day. She will be in the hospital for a long time because she weighs less than two pounds. Mama let me name her Felise. I can hardly wait to bring her home.*

Today the Patrol Force meeting is long. As usual, I am the last to leave because I like to stay around and talk with James Outlaw. I am sure he knows that. He has to know how much I love him. Has to. But it is not his style to make me feel bad about it. He stuffs his papers into a notebook and says to me, "So…what did you think of the meeting?"

"Kinda long." I tilt my head towards the window. "It's dark already."

"Where do you live?"

"Viola Street."

"Oh? May I walk you home?"

I feel my heart jump. I am so nervous I want to throw up. I can kick myself when I shrug my shoulders and say, "I don't care."

He takes me by the arm and leads me out of the room, across the school yard. I am sorry I live so close to the school. It is a clear, crisp evening. Smells of supper penetrate my nose as we walk past the small row of houses on my street. We talk about the stars, the moon, and the early evening quiet. At the edge of my yard we stop walking and he says, "Do you mind if I ask you a personal question?"

I am disgusted. I think it is beneath him. Boys my own age have no problem with walking up to me and asking that question. I am sick of hearing it. Now, with Pop about to ask me, I am more than a little annoyed and very disappointed that he could not think of anything original to say. I fold my arms in front of me. "Oh, now you're going to ask me if I am a virgin, right?"

He grimaces, knots his brows and leans his head to one side. "No...No!"

I feel like an idiot. "Ok. Well. What then?"

"Never mind." He places both hands over his heart and bows. "Mademoiselle, vous m'avez donne beaucoup de peine."

I laugh a little. He laughs a little. Then we both laugh a lot. My books fall to the ground and we laugh more. Tears run from my eyes. My sides hurt. Every time we try to stop laughing, we look at each other and start all over again. And then, as the laughter quiets to an embarrassed chuckle, James Outlaw kisses me on my mouth.

I do not wrap my arms around his neck. I do not swing back my leg and stand on one foot. I stand there frozen, melted, frozen again. The kiss is more delightful than a ride on a Ferris wheel. I am dizzy, suspended, the world spins around me. He tastes like spearmint. The soft warmth from his nostrils caresses my upper lip. His tongue slips gently into my mouth and I welcome it. I feel as if my blood has been drained and replaced with helium.

He cups my chin in his hand. "So," he says, "How old are you?"

six

By the time I got around to answering Pop's question he had already guessed, but he came to visit me anyway. Mama let me see him on Wednesday and Sunday evenings as long as Daddy wasn't at home. She and I both knew what would happen if he ever knew that truth. It worked pretty well, though. Daddy didn't come home every week, but when he did, he would come in late Friday night, and he would leave about five o'clock on Sunday. Pop would come over at six and stay until eleven.

I *loved* kissing him. That's about all we ever did. There was no television in the living room, and I was too immature to carry on a decent conversation. As soon as he sat down I reached over to kiss him. Every once in a while we'd come up for air, but we mostly kissed for the five hours he was there.

It never occurred to me how all that kissing affected a seventeen year-old hormonal male. I think about it now and wonder how he dealt with our relationship. Maybe he knew that I still saw sex as something nasty. I was still a kid to him and, in fact, that's what he calls me today. Kid. Maybe it was his over-abundance of chivalry and honor. Whatever it was, for the three years we courted, he never even brought up the subject. If he had sex with other girls he'd tell me about it. My childish mentality was set: *"Well, as long as you don't get it from me…"*

But the routine came to a screeching halt in August, 1959. Pop was leaving for university. Daddy just happened to be at home that weekend. So when Pop showed up unexpectedly at three in the afternoon, I was surprised and happy to see him, but I knew I had to tell Daddy. "Wait a minute," I said to Pop, and I braced myself for my father's wrath.

"Daddy," I said, trying to be casual and feeling for a non-existent pocket in my skirt. "There's a boy on the porch that I really like. He's going off to college tomorrow and I want you to meet him."

"What's his name?"

"Um…James Outlaw."

"Well is he an outlaw?"

"No sir."

"Well bring him on in here, then."

"Yes, sir."

I rushed to the door to get the man I adored and I led him by the hand to my parent's room. "This is my father," I said.

They shook hands. "Nice to meet you Mr. Williams. Good afternoon Mrs. Williams."

When Pop addressed Mama, I thought there would be trouble. He was acknowledging that he'd met her before. The secret was no longer a secret. But Daddy just said, "Y'all go on over across the hall, *but* leave the door open."

❊ ❊ ❊

I worked after school at Ingram's Drug Store. Dr. Ingram and her daughter Carol were very kind to me. They let me drink as many milkshakes as I could hold. I was five feet, seven inches tall, and I weighed ninety-three pounds. Carol would steam a hot dog for me and put chili on it. I suppose this was their way of giving me proper nutrition.

On Saturdays I worked at Wilson Variety Store from nine in the morning until nine at night. The money helped Mama pay the bills, and it also came in handy for my little incidentals. I used to go uptown to Mother and Daughter Department Store and put a lot of stuff on lay-away. Then I'd pay a few dollars a week until I could bring them home. This is how I bought my clothes. In 1960 you could get a nice pleated skirt for two dollars. A decent sweater for four.

Those of us who were fashion aware paid attention to and copied the kids who spent their summers in New York. The style for that year was *Bohemian*. We wore short, black skirts and tops, black stockings, Queen Anne shoes. We shaved our eyebrows and drew lines upward towards the scalp. We coated our faces with powder fives shades too light, and we wore no lipstick. You could not tell us we weren't fly. We were young and cool, a generation of hippy intellectuals, truly conscious of our identities. The voters were about to elect a president who promised to make changes for the betterment of all Americans. Dr. Martin Luther King, Jr. would show him how.

Miss Bonner, the school counselor, was determined to do her part. She arranged to take a group of us to Atlantic Christian College, an all-white institution on the west side of town. She made the boys wear ties and suits; she made the girls wear church dresses and high heels. She also made us wear white gloves. Before we went, she trained us all about how to be *polite* to white people. We had after-school sessions that involved walking with books on our heads to force us to stand up straight. There were lessons about how to sit with our hands in our laps, legs crossed at the ankle. We needed to walk stiffly, she said, no elaborate swing of the hips, no jiggling breasts. We should smile broadly when introduced, and above all, do not say anything about the Civil Rights Movement.

I don't remember much about that day. Most of us were like zombies--automatons going through the motions by rote. But I do remember the reaction of the receiving administration. They were overly friendly with liquid smiles that seemed painful. Many of the students stared at us, so much so that I felt uncomfortable. The rest simply ignored us.

I am certain that Miss Bonner had a purpose for that day, but what I learned from it was the recognition of the huge gap between them and us. Indeed there was a difference, and we were on the wrong side of that difference. My aunt Doretta had twelve children. Most of them were about my color: caramel. But four of them were albino—white with blond hair and blue eyes. So, white didn't excite me, and I had a difficult time trying to pretend that I enjoyed our little excursion.

I was glad when it was time to go. How many times can you answer stupid questions like, *What's your favorite subject in school? What do you want to be when you grow up? What do you do for fun?*

"My favorite subject is French."

"Oh? Vous parlez francais?"

"Oui. J'etudie avec Madame Marian Miller."

End of conversation.

"I want to be an interpreter at the UN."

Laughter. End of conversation.

"I go to socials at the Center on Friday nights."

"What else?"

What the hell did he mean by "what else?" I worked. And I studied. There wasn't much in between. Besides, the Center was it for us. We didn't have bowling alleys or skating rinks. We didn't have house parties, pool parties or outdoor barbeques. About the best we could do was Ingram's Drug Store for ice cream, Diggs Grill for jukebox music, Woodard's Inn for a really great hamburger, and The Stoplight Grill for Sunday gatherings, all of which were once-in-a-while events.

By the time we got back to our side of town I was exhausted. It takes a lot of energy to front like that. I went to my room, stripped off all the pretense and went to bed, grateful for the return of normalcy.

seven

Mrs. Johnnie B. Harris was my Home Economics teacher. She was also bacillus of the local chapter of Delta Sigma Theta Sorority. It was they who sponsored the annual Debutante Ball. One day, in the fall of my junior year at Darden, Mrs. Harris asked me to wait after class. She held an envelope in her hand and said, "I don't know how this could possibly have happened. Your name was not on the list of girls chosen to be debutantes. I apologize for this late notice, but here is your invitation."

There was no need for an apology; I had been busy working and chasing Mr. Fitch, the mailman, hoping for a letter from Pop. I didn't even notice the excitement around campus. The ball was scheduled for the following spring. It included girls with good reputations from Wilson and Rocky Mount, and the Deltas were planning a week of activities for us like dances, dinner parties, theater parties, lessons on charm and etiquette. I would have to invite a boy to be my escort. By that time I would be sixteen. The ball would be my first formal, and I would need a beautiful white gown. I couldn't wait to tell Mama.

"Ain't no way I can do that," she said. "Wiley ain't sent no money in months. We need all you can make and all I can make just to get by."

I was heart-broken. And angry. My mother was always too eager to surrender. Sometimes I felt like the stork must have been on drugs when he dropped me off in that family. I started to reflect on the way things had been. While my friends were outside playing, I worked. At seven years old I was already breaking boundaries that were set before me by someone else. By ten, I had two jobs. When my sister came home from the hospital, I was teaching Bible school, but I had to quit to take care of her. Now, with my boyfriend hundreds of miles away, I felt like I was alone in the world. We were so unlike each other, Mama and I. I was never one to be deterred by a negative answer, but it looked like negativity was all that she expected. I was hurt when I went to bed that night. With a childhood that ended much too quickly, I realized that I had to create a life for myself, and I thought about all the possible ways I could make the Debutante Ball happen for me.

I awoke with a plan. I went to Lucille's Bridal Shop uptown on Nash Street. I looked through the gorgeous gowns in the store for a long time. At last I found the perfect one. It was pure white, strapless with a net shawl. It had a fitted bodice with rows and rows of lace in the back, and each row had a white satin bow. The dress cost sixty-two dollars. I asked the clerk if I could try it on. She showed me to the fitting room. She wanted to see the dress on me. When I came out wearing it she said, "It looks like it was made for you."

I asked to speak with her mother, the owner of the shop. The clerk led me to the back room. Miss Lucille was a tall, heavy set woman with dyed black hair. She sat at a desk eating a cheese sandwich. She offered me a bite, but I said, "No thank you." She slurped cream of tomato soup and asked if I wanted some of that. I didn't. Then she said, "What can I do for you?"

"I want…I *need* this dress," I said. "But I don't have any money. If you give me a job, I'll work and pay it off. I'm willing to do anything."

She stared me up and down for a few seconds. She polished an apple with her skirt and took a bite. She wore a funny kind of smile that's hard to describe. At last she said, "Can you start today?"

"Oh yes ma'am. I can start right now. Right now!"

❀ ❀ ❀

At first my job was to dust the plastic garment covers that protected the gowns, and to sweep and mop the floor. After a while, though, I became the salesperson for all the *colored* girls who came into the shop. I worked hard, and Miss Lucille finally coaxed me into eating cheese sandwiches and tomato soup on my break. We had a solid relationship. That woman was good to me. When we talked, it was more than employer/employee instructions. We actually had conversations and I learned a lot from her about history, slavery and the Holocaust. She taught me about the strength and survival of women in a male-dominant corporate world. She urged me to travel away from Wilson and learn other cultures before I decided to settle down.

I paid off my dress long before the ball, and I continued to work for her. In that way, I was able to buy everything I needed for the week-long activities. I even bought a dress for Mama and new Sunday shoes and clothes for my little brother and sister.

I invited Braxton McPhail to be my escort, and he accepted. That was something new for both of us. Nice girls generally waited for the boy to say

37

something to them, but this was different. I knew he had a girlfriend, but it wasn't about that. It was about finding a good, clean, intelligent and wholesome guy to take me to this very special dance and present me to the world. That described Brat to a tee.

The day of the ball arrived. I got up early to do my chores. At noon I heard the whistle blow at Export Tobacco factory. It was time for me to start getting ready. I went to Vivian James' house because her mother was the best hairdresser in town. I had what we called "blow hair," and Mrs. James was the only one I knew who could straighten and curl it just right. Everybody else either burned my hair or forehead, or they made me look like a stick doll with a plastic mane. Mrs. James gave me an "upsweep"…a lot of little curls piled high on my head. As soon as I got home I tore a paper bag and rolled my hair before I took my bath so my "do" wouldn't fall. I shaved my arm pits and arched my brows. I put on my brand new panties and stuffed my strapless bra with tissue. I inhaled excitement, and when Aunt Aileen came from Durham and brought me her Mouton jacket to wear, I felt like Cinderella.

Mama helped me tie on the hoop slip and she zipped my gown. Then, I put on the white satin shoes I had bought the day before. I filled the matching clutch bag with lipstick and a handkerchief. Next, I put on my pearl earrings and necklace, and my white formal length gloves. A squirt of Evening in Paris perfume and I was ready for Braxton. When I sat down, the front of my dress flew up and showed everything Mother Nature had given me. Mama laughed. She told me that the hoop slip was the culprit. "You have to sit in formal gowns like this, not on them," she said. And she taught me how to raise the dress from behind before I sat down. I was so glad to have had that experience at home.

The Export whistle blew again. It was five o'clock. The ball was in Rocky Mount, and we had to be there at six. For a fleeting moment I was nervous, afraid that Braxton wouldn't come. The parents had to deliver the girls to the ball, but the boys were allowed to take us home. My mother's friend, Mrs. Mary Godwin, drove us, and when we arrived, Braxton was already there. He helped me out of the car and presented me with a wrist corsage of red carnations. Oh, he was soooo handsome! He extended his arm. Together we walked proudly into the ballroom where we lined up for presentation.

It was a mystical, magical night. Braxton held me gently as we waltzed. Years later I would learn that his sister had taught him that dance the previous day. His mother had worked overtime to buy his tuxedo. And he was deliriously happy that I had invited him. We danced all night. There were other names on my dance card and I obliged, but I noticed that Braxton only danced with me. My new shoes rubbed blisters on my feet and I kept on dancing. Photographer lights flashed every way we turned. For at least this one night I felt like a princess. I was, in fact, Miss Barbara Ann Williams, from Wilson.

❀   ❀   ❀

The following year was tense. News of racial violence in the southern states became headlines for every major newspaper in the country. Sit-ins in Greensboro, North Carolina had begun at Woolworth's in 1960. Fire bombings of churches in Birmingham, Alabama caused the town to become known as "Bombingham." Fire hoses and dogs were turned on black people in Birmingham and Little Rock, Arkansas. Stories of Emmett Till's murder were told and re-told in schools and churches as warnings to be careful. Death and violence escalated to the point that the president and his brother got involved and took action. They sent federal marshals into Montgomery, Alabama to quell the violence. Late in the year, they sent federal marshals and troops into Oxford, Mississippi to integrate Ole Miss. Both black and white Freedom Riders had been killed, but Dr. King and Mrs. Rosa Parks were held as heroes in the black community.

Bombing churches was a habit of the Klan and they obviously thought it was an effective one. The church was the only place that blacks could meet. It brought people together under the protective umbrella of spirituality. Without the church, the *unit* of people became disintegrated. But just as necessity was the mother of invention, it was also the foundation of innovation. People called meetings at schools, the Center, each other's homes.

I went home for lunch one day and turned on the television. There was an angry white man who said something I never forgot: "I got news for you niggers…you niggers. You say you're on the move. Well we're on the move, too! That's right. I don't believe in segregation. I believe in slavery!" This one statement made me think that the movement was worthwhile. The man sounded angry, but I saw something else in his eyes: fear. I felt joy that was almost pain. I believed that things would get worse before they got better, but because of that man, I was hopeful.

Letters from Pop were slow coming. He'd send a few words to let me know that he was all right, busy working and studying hard. But the glorious words of love he used to write were absent. Mama had told me that he would find somebody else in college. She told me to write him and tell him to be safe and not get involved in any of the *mess* that was going on in the country. I did. A letter came from him almost immediately. He wrote: "It is not mess! It is an important mark in our history, and we are proud." Within the week I received another letter from him. He no longer wanted to be my boyfriend.

I AM SEVENTEEN YEARS OLD. In a month I will graduate from high school. I should be happy, but all I do is cry. My grades are slipping. I take my mother's advice and, in the process, I lose the man I love. I am so mad at her. I should have known better than to listen to her advice about what to say to a man. Even her own man can't stand to be around her, and he makes babies with another woman. Sometimes, when he is in town, I see him with his girlfriend and their little boy. Mama knows about it, but she does nothing. I could kick myself for listening to her.

I don't know what this is. Nothing interests me anymore. I don't want to go to school or work. I have no appetite. No energy. I don't have a fever or runny nose, but I feel so sick. I don't feel alive. I wish I could go outside and let the sun evaporate me. I avoid the crowds of elated seniors. They are all so happy with their promises of bright futures. They have celebration parties, but I don't go. They meet at Digg's Grill, but I don't go there, either. I stay locked up in my room. I pray for rain, a flood even, so I can go outside and drown.

eight

I slowly began to emerge from my discomfort over losing Pop. I worked all that summer in green tobacco. I could not save any money because my family was so needy. I had been accepted at North Carolina College in Durham. Aunt Aileen lived around the corner from the campus and she took in student boarders. She would not let me stay with her because I was a girl; she only wanted boys because they were less trouble. College was my planned route of escape from Wilson. The bus was to leave at five in the evening. It was a Sunday. At four, Mama sat me down and told me that I could not go. She didn't have any money, and she needed me to work and help with the bills.

I think I felt pain at this revelation, but I also felt a kind of numbness. I was trapped. Most of my friends went off to college, even those who were not terribly smart. Some of them got married. The rest took off for places like New York, Baltimore, Washington, D. C. and Philadelphia. There I was, stuck in Wilson with little hope of getting out.

I got a job as a maid for a family on Thurston Drive. Both the parents were laborers. He was a plumber; she worked at a rubber company. There were two children, a ten year old boy and a seven year old girl. It was my job to take care of them, clean the house, do the laundry, and cook lunch and dinner. I made fourteen dollars a week.

Mrs. Morris drove a raggedy car that trembled whenever she reached sixty miles an hour. This happened often as she was always in a hurry to pick me up before she went to work. My first day on the job brought disappointment. Their furniture was no better than ours. Their refrigerator was empty most of the time. She introduced me to her kids as "Our new girl," and her husband hollered and cussed her, right in front of me.

I worked for them for almost a year. I knew that I couldn't do that for very long. I was too smart for it. Too ambitious, and much too rebellious. A neighbor helped me get into Livingstone College in Salisbury, North Carolina. My cousin, Earnest, lived in Neptune, New Jersey. He invited me to come stay with him for the summer so I could work and save money for school. As

Zora Neale Hurston once said, "I was going to wrassle myself up a future or die trying." So, on May 18, 1963, I boarded a bus and headed north.

Earnest's wife's name was Betty. At first I thought our relationship would be strained, but she treated me well. She loved to sew, and she made clothes for me. The tension was between the two of them; somehow they just couldn't seem to get it all together. They had three children at the time, two girls and a boy. They did not charge me rent; my only chore was to wash dishes.

I got a job as a checker at Shop-Rite Grocery Store in Oakhurst. Earnest would take me to work in the mornings and pick me up after my shift. I made a dollar and twenty-five cents an hour, and I brought home fifty-four dollars a week. That was big money for someone who didn't have to pay rent or buy groceries. Earnest deposited the fifty into his bank account and gave me the four as an allowance. By the end of the summer I had saved over five hundred dollars.

But something happened on my first day at Shop-Rite that would change my life forever. I met a boy. He had a long and formal name, and eventually I would start calling him Hubbie, so let's call him that now. He was the only black male employee at the store, and I was the only girl. He was sweet and respectful, and it just seemed like the most natural thing to say "yes" when he asked me out on a date.

He drove a 1958 white Chevrolet Impala. He was the only boy I ever knew who owned a car. He took me to MacDonald's and to a drive-in movie. When he took me home we stayed in the car and talked for a long time. After a while I realized that it was five o'clock in the morning. I didn't have a key, so I had to ring the bell to get into my cousin's apartment. Earnest was furious. "A boy that will keep you out until five in the morning will never marry you," he said.

I wasn't even thinking about marriage. I thought I had a lot of living to do, a lot of growing up to do before anything like that could happen. Besides, I didn't feel that way about Hubbie. I was still in love with Pop. My greatest ambition in life was to marry Pop, curl up under him every night, give him a baby for every year, and after a dozen or so, flutter my lashes, look towards the window and die peacefully in his arms.

I didn't know it then, but Pop had set a paradigm and I measured every man in my life against it. No man, not even my husbands, would ever be able to take his place, and I told them that at the beginning. Their mistake lay in believing that they could change my mind.

Still, it was a good summer. Hubbie took me to the beach and the board-walk in Asbury Park. We haunted Long Branch and Red Bank. Once in a while we'd visit Uncle Elmer and his family who were stationed in Hazlet. One time we even went to the Brooklyn Fox Theater to see Marvin Gaye. I was beginning to understand the expansiveness of the world.

At the end of the summer I prepared to leave. Hubbie gave me his telephone number and permission to call collect. I promised to write. The folks on my job were disappointed that I was leaving. They thought I wanted to be a permanent employee. They did, however, wish me well, and I was finally on my way to wholeness.

nine

I absolutely hated Livingstone College. Freshman Hell Night was exactly that, pure hell. Some of my classmates from Darden were sophomores already. Their air of superiority annoyed me to no end. Freshman women occupied the third floor of Gohler Hall. Sophomores were on the second floor and Juniors were on the first. The sophomores and juniors woke us up in the middle of the second night. They made us stand at attention. Most of us slept in our panties and bras or a half slip pulled up over our breasts. I felt naked to the world.

They talked to us like they were Marine Corp Gunneries. One girl cried. When they got to me, Anita, bacillus of Alpha Kappa Alpha, said to me: "I hear you think you can sing. Why don't you sing something for us?" I stumbled over a couple of notes of something by the Supremes. They all laughed. Then I started to sing the alma mater: "Oh Livingstone. My Livingstone…" The rest of the freshman class joined in and the upper classmen left me alone.

Over the next few weeks I would come to think of Anita as rude, brash, vulgar and just about everything else negative one can imagine. She walked too fast with her slippers slapping against the heels of her feet. She strutted like she owned the campus. There was always an entourage following her, and she was the boss, no doubt about that. She had a laugh that was way too loud, and she spread her mouth wide enough to reveal one gold tooth and one missing one. Anita was from New York City. Her boyfriend's name was Jack, and on more than one occasion I heard her tell him: "Mother fucker get behind me where you belong." When she learned that I would major in French, she let me borrow her text book. Every time she saw me she'd say, "Barbara Williams, gimme my damn book!"

But I accidentally learned that all that harshness was a cover for Anita's deep vulnerability. My roommate was crazy. I mean really crazy. She was nasty with her body and she was nasty with our room. She kicked the door open so many times that it would fly open at the least movement in the hall. She had an odor about her that would not quit, and she never, ever, took a bath. Sometimes she'd wear the same clothes for days. She even slept in them. Whenever she did change her clothes she left them piled in a corner on the floor. Once in a while she'd pick something up and put it on. In all the time I roomed with her she never went to the Laundromat. I complained to the RA, who spoke with Mrs. Johnson, the house monitor. A bed had become vacant on the junior floor because a girl got pregnant and was sent home. I was given permission to move into that room, and Anita was one of its occupants.

I came in from class one day and caught her crying. She was the toughest young woman I had ever met, next to Grandma Easter. I used to listen to her counsel other girls in the dorm: "You got to take care of self. Ain't nothing wrong with kissin'. I loves it myself. A'int nothing' wrong with screwin' neither. Only difference is, I do mine in a bed and you do yours on a table in the library." And I'll never forget the time she said to Jack: "Look, Sweetie, why did you do it? Because you wanted to, right? Your first obligation is to your damned self. So, why worry about how I feel about it?" This crying, then, was so out of character for her.

"What's the matter?"

She put up her hand and waved me off.

"Come on," I said. "You can tell me. What happened?"

She could barely get it out between sobs. Jack had broken up with her. He said she didn't respect him, and he wasn't going to put up with it any longer.

I put my arms around her and hugged her tightly. She cried herself to sleep. I cried, too. I could actually feel her pain.

Anita and I became good friends after that. She taught me how to play Bid Whist and Pinochle. She gave me intimate details about her love sessions with Jack and how she missed them. And she protected me from the bullies in Gohler Hall who were pissed because I roomed with the juniors.

She talked about sex a lot. She and the other girls in our room shared information about Emko, a foam contraceptive, rubbers, and first-time friction. The more I heard, the more convinced I was to try it. I went to New Jersey for spring break.

◈　◈　◈

By this time I was nineteen years old. Hubbie picked me up from the bus station and we spent the entire week together. In all that time he didn't seem to be aware of why I was there. So, on the morning of the last day of my visit, I indicated that sex was an experience I wanted to have.

I was staying with Pearl, Uncle Elmer's ex-wife. I put on some music and gently led Hubbie to my room. I was too shy to get undressed, so I kept on my pajamas and got into bed. I wiggled my finger for him to join me, which he eagerly did.

It was a disaster. He tried to put his thing in that place where only Dr. Cowan's finger had been. It didn't work. I stiffened. I said to myself, "I do not like this. This shit hurts." He came on my thigh before anything serious could happen. "You excite me too quick," he said. I went back to Livingstone, still a virgin.

✺ ✺ ✺

At the end of the school year I determined to go back to the grocery store in New Jersey and work for the summer. My cousin was angry because I had not written. This meant that I had to find a place to live. My full-time job was gone, so I took part-time whenever I could get it. I found a furnished room in Asbury Park that cost ten dollars a week. For the first few nights I had to sleep in Hubbie's car because I didn't have any money. Later, I borrowed the money from Uncle Elmer and moved into my room. With paying for my room, transportation to and from work and buying my own food, I could not save anything for a second year at Livingstone. I only had thirty hours a week most of the time. Mama and Daddy were having a hard time, so I decided to work for a year and then go to Monmouth College. I would help them all I could.

Even though Hubbie worked at night and I worked during the day, we still managed to spend time together. Most of that time was in my room at the boarding house, and well, one thing led to another and we settled into a very comfortable and safe relationship. He used to buy things for me—a bracelet, a radio, something to wear—just because. I liked the attention. I also liked being his girl. He loved to show me off to his friends and brag about me being a college student. Towards the end of the summer we stopped at a jewelry store and he bought a set of diamond rings. He put them in his pocket and we got into the car and drove off. When we stopped at a traffic light he handed one of them to me and said, "Here."

I don't know what I was thinking. I'm not even sure I *was* thinking. But I took the ring and wore it proudly.

He started coming to my place every day after that. He'd pick me up from work and stay until it was time for him to go. Then he'd come when

46

his shift was over and stay until time to take me to back to work. We played all the grown-up games. The only trouble was neither of us knew the rules very well. So we improvised, and by December I was pregnant.

Everything changed. I was sick every morning, too sick to go to work. I eventually quit my job and Hubbie had to pay for everything. I didn't know what to do about my problem. I tried to wish it away; I tried praying it away. When it became apparent that the baby was locked in and determined to get here, we talked about getting married. But I was only nineteen and he was twenty. In those days the boy had to be twenty-one to get married without parental permission. He did not want his mother to have to sign for him. So we waited. And the baby grew.

We began to argue about little things. Most of the time he'd say what he had to say and then leave and go stay with his mother for two or three days. Once I accused him of not caring about me because he'd stopped buying me presents. He said, "I had to. I can't do everything. If you hadn't got yourself in trouble I could still buy shit."

Another time he tried to pay me a compliment by low rating his ex-girlfriend. He just came into my room and sat down. The first thing out of his mouth was, "I saw Blossom today."

"Really? Where?"

"At her house. I went to see her brother."

"Funny how you never see her when I'm with you."

"What you trying to say?"

"Nothing."

"I don't know what I ever saw in that girl. Dumb as toast. Don't know shit from gravy. I had to teach her everything." He smiled a little then. "'Cept how to fuck. I sure didn't have to teach her how to fuck."

I was deeply offended. "I don't want to hear about that!" I said.

"What you getting all excited for?"

"You make me feel like she can do that better than I can!"

"Aw, you always gotta take things the wrong way!"

He shoved his way past me and left that time, too. I cried for three days. I didn't think he would ever come back. When he did, I was so glad to see him that I avoided talking about what happened.

If I had had any sense, any sense at all, I would have recognized that moment as a foreshadowing of what was to come and I would have stayed single. I would not be the first girl to get pregnant before marriage and I certainly wouldn't be the last. But the thought of going home to my mother with a baby in tow was a terrifying one. And my father's voice kept echoing in my mind: "You just like your damn mama. Fast." So I stayed and took whatever Hubbie was willing to give me.

In June of 1965, Hubbie was inducted into the Army. The first word in the letter was "Congratulations." He'd have to do eight weeks of boot camp and then surely go off to Vietnam. I'd be stuck there alone with a baby after all. I couldn't think past my own situation and I told him so: "I don't know what I'm going to do without you here."

And he said, "Maybe I won't have to go. I went down to the recruitment office today and I told them you are pregnant and that we are getting married on Monday. He said all I have to do is bring the marriage license to him."

Sure enough, by ten o'clock Monday morning I was a married woman. Hubbie's mother signed for him.

ten

Our first daughter was born in September of that year. We had another one two years later. Hubbie was disappointed that we did not have a son, and he blamed me for it until his mother told him that the man determines the sex of a child.

The marriage was a good one for a while. It required work, but I had made a commitment and I would stand by it. Mama used to say, "Remember, it's for life." So I tried to be a good wife even when I didn't feel like it. Hubbie demanded sex every night and some mornings. There was no spontaneity, no emotion, no foreplay. Just a quick poking and a rollover. If I refused to do that chore, he'd get mad and would not speak for a few days.

I cried a lot during that marriage. Don't get me wrong; there were plenty of good times. But there was always the lingering threat that I would do or say something that would make him angry. Except for an occasional restaurant, I cooked every meal we ate. I did all the laundry and helped the kids with school work. I made all our clothes, even his suits. I was content, but I was unsettled, unanchored. I went through the motions of life, but I felt left out of the living. I felt empty, unfulfilled. I had been taking care of kids and a house all my life and I still managed to do other things. I needed adult conversation and intellectual stimulation, and Hubbie was pitifully inadequate in that regard.

I wanted to go back to college. We tried to make plans for that but there was always something standing in the way. We needed a new car, a new washing machine, a bigger house, and money was an issue. There never seemed to be time or money enough for me to go to school. Yet, without an education, I could not earn enough to keep us out of trouble.

I decided to get a license in real estate to help us become financially stable enough to allow me to return to college. I got a job making dental drills to pay for the course. I worked from ten at night until six in the morning. Hubbie was on swing shift and we only had one car. He'd come to pick me up from work and, when he was on day shift, I'd drop him off at his job. Then I'd take the kids to school and go home to get some sleep.

I went to class from one until five in the afternoons. Hubbie would ride home with his car pool. Then I would make dinner, help the kids with their homework, go back to bed until nine and then get up and go to work again.

I thought it was a workable routine. The course only lasted for six weeks. After that all I had to do was pass the state boards and get a job somewhere.

Because of my schedule, Hubbie was home alone with the children two out of every three weeks. I got off work at six o'clock in the morning and, after a few days he began to come late to drive me home. It got later and later until finally I arranged to get a ride with another employee. On the first day, Hubbie was in bed. Said he'd overslept. But on the second day, I got home an hour before he did. I could tell that he'd been at the bar. Not that he was a drinker; he didn't drink or smoke. But he did like to socialize with the patrons of the corner bar. Even so, the bar closed at two a. m. and he smelled of stale musk oil and cigarettes. Naturally, I was curious, so I questioned him about it.

"Jessie was in the bar, right?"

"Yeah, how'd you know."

"I can smell her perfume on you."

"Well. I'll have to tell Jessie that she got me in trouble."

"No…you're not in trouble. I'd just like to know where my children are."

"I took them to my mother's."

"Why?"

"Because I'm tired of babysitting! That's why."

Now, that's something I've never been able to understand. How does a man see taking care of his own children as *babysitting?* When people say, "It takes a village to raise a child," why are all the villagers women? We didn't make them by ourselves. It all seems so unfair.

※　※　※

I finished the course, passed the state exams and got a job immediately in Willingboro, New Jersey. It was an hour and a half down the turnpike. I was often late getting home. Normally, Hubbie and the kids were not there, so I'd run in and make dinner, then go to the bar to get them. But on this one day he *was* there, and he was mad as hell. He sat at the kitchen table with his fists to his temple.

"What's the matter with you?" I asked.

His look was hard. "I'm hungry!"

"Okay, I'm going to make dinner right now. I'm sorry I'm late, but you know I have to work."

"You don't have to work! You just *want* to!"

I felt the need to remind him of why I was working in the first place. "Hubbie, we need the money so I can go back to college."

"Oh why the hell you want to go to college anyway? You already got a husband!"

So that was it. His reluctance to support my educational pursuits was by design. Instantly I started to reflect on all the times the word "college" entered our conversation, and I began to realize that his masculinity was threatened by the notion. I could feel the storm brewing inside of me, and I could anticipate the same in him. It had been a good day at the office and I did not want to argue. We were doing well. We even had money in the bank.

"Honey…" I said, "make a sandwich and go watch TV. Dinner will be ready soon."

"Aw, why I gotta make my own sandwich? That's what I got a wife for! I paid three dollars for you, and you need to do your damn job!"

With that he pushed away from the table and left. I could hear the tires screeching as he left the parking lot. His words were a revelation, though. He believed he owned me. I didn't remember signing over property rights when I signed the marriage license. I remembered the "for better or worse part," and I thought that with me working and bringing home my money, that should be better. I also remembered the "to love and to cherish." But didn't he also make those same promises? Why was it that when he stopped speaking to me I was the one who had to make up? Why did my job threaten him so much?

I was confused. I realized that we never took the time to sit down and define our roles. We never discussed what we expected from each other. We'd been married over seven years and I was just finding out that making his sandwich was a part of my job. I thought about the little things he had said or done over the years concerning the role of a wife and I put them all together that day. A wife should be at home when her husband comes in from work or *wherever*. She should have his dinner ready, his clothes clean. The children should be neat, happy and out of his way. She should be supportive of his every whim. Be prepared to feed an army at a moment's notice. She must wait on him hand and foot. Nurse him when he is sick. Be happy for him when he is successful in some venture. Pity him when he is weak. She must serve up steak at least once a week. Keep the kids in Osh

51

Kosh and Buster Browns, pay the rent, the light bill, buy groceries and make travel arrangements—all on $157 a week. And *if* he lets her get a job, she should be a file clerk or something so that he will have the larger income, and she won't be so tired when she comes home that she can't do anything for him. If he lets her have a job, she should be satisfied with a little old raggedy car. He has to drive the good car because, after all, he has the bigger salary. And when the income tax refund comes, *he* decides what to do with it because either he's the only one working or her little money doesn't do anything but buy curtains anyway. A wife should accept her lot. Be content with whatever her husband can provide for her. Above all, she should be eager and willing to let him pound her into the mattress every night.

❀   ❀   ❀

I noticed that Jessie was always in the neighborhood when I came home from work. She was my friend. When Hubbie was on the evening shift, she'd come over and bring a bottle of V. O. We'd laugh and talk about the crazy things people were doing down at the bar. Jessie was tall, brown, rather boyish-looking with her square hips. She had huge breasts and a big gap between her front teeth. She could beat every one of the guys on the pool table. We were completely opposite, but there was something about her that I liked. She reminded me of Anita. Maybe it was her toughness on the outside and her vulnerability on the inside. She used to sit and talk about her mysterious and often absent man. She kept my glass full of V. O. until I couldn't do anything but go to bed. It never occurred to me that those were the nights Hubbie didn't come home.

For months I had been getting a lot of play from the men at the bar. I thought it was because I sold real estate and dressed up all the time. Hell, I looked good. I did. At twenty-seven years old I was what you might call *mega-fine*. So, though I was pleased that they all had nice things to say, I wasn't flattered. They were simply telling the truth. To me, there was nothing more appealing than an honest man. But then they started saying things like "Hubbie's a fool. If I had a woman like you I'd stay home every night." I was so stupid, I'd go right home and tell him what they said and who said it. When one of them tried to tell me that Hubbie had a girlfriend I said to him, "Oh no. Not Hubbie. My husband would never do a thing like that."

I started having bad dreams. One was about snakes. The way I was raised, if you dream about snakes you have enemies. As far as I could tell

I hadn't done anything that would make anybody hate me. But I dreamed that snakes were crawling all over my bed. Hundreds of them. Black ones, yellow ones, striped and polka dotted snakes crawled from the floor to the bed, all over my legs, my face and across my belly. They seemed so real. I jumped out of bed and shook the sheet. "Get up, Honey! Get up! There are snakes in the bed!" Hubbie raised up on one elbow and said, "Well…don't shake them over here on me."

The dream worried me and I couldn't sleep in the bed anymore. I took to sleeping on the sofa. There I had a dream that would repeat itself periodically over the next eight or nine years. A dream that, ultimately, saved my life. A man with a large gun chased me. I was at an apartment complex that was shaped like a U. I ran down one side, across the open end, and down the other side. There were some galvanized tin garbage cans, three of them, lined up against the wall next to a sliding glass door. I tripped over the cans and fell into them. The man stood over me with the gun pointed at my face and, just as he pulled the trigger, I woke up. Every time.

I didn't know what either of the dreams meant, but I knew that something was going on. Besides, Hubbie had always been an every night lover. If I was not in the mood for sex, he'd take it. Now, weeks would pass without any contact. I decided that it was time for us to talk about it. So, when I came home from work early one evening and he was not there, I went to the bar to look for him.

He wasn't there, of course. But a girl I knew said that she would help me find him. She led me to places in Long Branch that I never knew existed and, no, we did not find Hubbie. Perhaps the dreams had frightened me, made me feel all alone. I don't know. Whatever I felt at that moment made me say something to her that surprised even me: "I know Hubbie has a girlfriend. I just don't know who it is." And she said, "It's Jessie."

I just about lost my mind. I don't remember dropping the girl off at her house. I don't remember driving to mine. I do remember kicking in the bedroom door and finding Hubbie asleep in the bed. I screamed at him for a long time while I packed my things. After telling him that I intended to leave there was only one thing I could say: "Jessie! Of all people. Jessie!" I must have said that a hundred times that night.

He tried to calm me but I wouldn't have it. Finally he said, "Well…go ahead and leave then. It's what you want to do anyway. Ever since you got that real estate license, all of a sudden I'm not good enough for you."

That made me stop and think. So it was my fault. All I ever wanted to do was have a better life for us and the kids. I did everything my old buddies in the dorm had told me to do. Played the "oooh baby you so good" role. Made him think he had enough to spare. Now that I was busy working and couldn't be at his beck and call, couldn't stroke his ego every time he needed it, he had to find someone who could. Oh, yeah. I got it. It was all my fault.

"Well at least we agree on something," he said. "Now all you have to do is quit that job and everything will be okay again." He offered to stop seeing Jessie if I would stay home and be happy with the life he could give me. Take care of our children like I was supposed to do. "She tricked me anyway," he said. "I was a lonely man and she took advantage of me. But don't take this as an excuse."

"You have no excuse."

"I wasn't talking about me. I mean don't take this as an excuse for you to go out and do something. Just because I was weak don't mean you have to be, too. Two wrongs don't make a right."

"I don't believe you. Is that all you can think about?"

"I guess I don't have to worry about it too much. Ain't nobody gonna mess with you. They all too scared of me."

That was early Sunday morning. On Tuesday evening he said to me, "I'm going crazy in this house. I have to go out for a while. Don't worry about me. I'm just going to ride along the beach. I'll be back in a little while."

As soon as he left I called a taxi. I searched the beach and all the bars. I looked everywhere I thought he might have gone, even stopped to ask a couple of people I knew if they had seen him. By the time I got back home he was already there.

"If I had known you'd go looking for me I woulda stayed the fuck home."

"Maybe that's what you should have done anyway. Keep your fat ass home with your family."

He reached for me and I ducked. Then he was gone again and I didn't see him until the next evening. After that I refused to let him out of my sight whenever we were not at work. I did not quit my job. But when I was at home, I expected him to be there, too.

I followed him wherever he went. One night we went to the bar and we were actually beginning to have a good time. It was family night so we took the kids. The old crowd was there and it was close to Christmas, so everyone was in a festive mood. I even laughed again. Just about time I got comfortable, in walked Jessie. A decent woman would have left as soon as she saw the two of us. Not her. She strolled down to the end of the bar and behaved in her same old loud, obscene manner. I told Hubbie that it was time for us to go and I stood up. He kept his seat. I stood back and said, "I'm

54

waiting. Are you coming or not?" He jumped off the bar stool with such a force that he knocked it over. He stormed past me and ran out to the car. I was in hot pursuit, dragging each of the girls by the hand.

We didn't say a word all the way home, but once we got there, it was on. He said I had embarrassed him. "We didn't have to leave!" he said.

"I don't want to be around her!"

"You make her think she's won!"

"Won what?! You're my own personal husband!"

With that I hauled off and slapped him in the face. The blow landed just at the tip of his nose. He hit me back and knocked me down. I got up swinging and he hit me again. I realized that I was no match for him, so I scrambled to a corner and stayed there. My children were crying and so was I. He was swollen with anger, and he stood over me with his fists clenched, taunting me to "Get up! Get the fuck up!"

I waited until he left and then I tried to comfort my daughters. We were all frightened because in nine years nothing like this had ever happened. I wanted to leave right then, but Christmas was less than a month away. I told myself that it was an isolated event. I had provoked him. I heard the voice of my mother again: *Remember, it's for life. For better or worse, it's for life.* I needed a plan to work this out. He had gone to Jessie to spite me, but now, he was in love with her. He didn't want to break up our family any more than I did. I should just be patient and understanding. It would work out by itself. Or, maybe it was all my fault. It was my responsibility to make it work. I had to be more loving. I had always said that I would walk away if he ever hit me. But I did hit him first, didn't I? Any animal will fight back when he is attacked. I had to make sure I didn't do that again.

eleven

Each year Hubbie and I had gone into debt to make sure the kids had a good Christmas because we were what you might call *deprived* when we were children. He was the youngest of fifteen kids; I knew the truth about Santa when I was very young. Normally, we started shopping for them in late October, but this year nothing had been done. I only went to the office when he was on day shift, so money was again a problem. About a week before Christmas Hubbie gave me eighty dollars and told me to explain to the kids that times were hard. The next day he came back and took a twenty. He said, "I need to have some money in my pocket, you know."

I couldn't buy dinner and presents on sixty dollars. So I went to the bank and applied for a loan of four hundred and fifty. It was instantly approved, but the loan officer needed my husband's signature. I got in my car and headed home. I knew that Hubbie would never sign that paper; we were already having so much financial trouble. When I stopped at the traffic light, I carefully signed his name on the line, making sure to dot the "i" with a small heart the way he did. It was a perfect forgery, and the man gave me the money. I convinced myself that there was nothing wrong with what I did. We were "as one" weren't we? I was Mrs. Hubbie, wasn't I? My kids deserved better than what we were giving them. It was not their fault. And when they said, "Thank you Mommy and Daddy," Hubbie said, "You're welcome." He never asked me where I got the money to buy presents.

I tried to make our holiday as festive as possible for the children. I cooked everything they liked, even though I didn't feel well. The backs of my legs ached, and there was an odor about me that I could not wash away. But Hubbie stayed home for Christmas and we actually got along again.

He had to work on New Year's Eve. Again, I cooked all day. I made Hopping John because black-eyed peas are supposed to bring good luck in the coming year. I also made some resolutions. One of them was to quit smoking. The other was to forgive him for Jessie. We could go into the new year and leave the past in the past. I took a bath and got all dressed up. He was due at 4:45. I'd have dinner ready and then we'd curl up by the fireplace and watch the snow fall. It was already six inches deep, so when I realized that Hubbie was late, I didn't worry much. Heavy snow always made them about an hour late.

But by six-thirty I did begin to worry. I kept running to the window every time I heard a car pass. Another hour slipped by. No Hubbie. I fed the kids and put them to bed. I called everyone in his car pool. They had all gotten home safely hours ago. I was out of cigarettes and I was worried out of my mind. What if something happened to him? What if he's wrapped around a tree somewhere, bleeding and helpless? My mind began to play tricks on me. Usually, if I thought about how rich I would be if he got killed, he'd come home. But that didn't work this time. I looked at my watch and it was after ten. I had not heard a word from him.

I called the bar. No, they had not seen Hubbie. Yes, they would tell him to bring me some cigarettes if he comes in. I could hear the celebration in the background. I hung up and called the state police. No, there had not been a report of an accident. I called the bar again and I could hear the crowd counting down. When they started singing Auld Lang Sine, I hung up the phone. For the first time in nine years I had missed welcoming in a new year with my husband. I couldn't understand it. Even people who hated each other could get together for a drink to toast in the new year. I was drinking alone. And I was very drunk.

It was Jessie. He had to be with Jessie.

I went to check on my children and they were sound asleep. Our house was situated in such a way that the back door opened to the parking area. He always came in that door. The room was a formal dining room, but since we had no furniture there, that area was empty. I went to the gun cabinet and took out a Remington .35. I loaded the rifle and placed a chair next to the wall that faced the back door. I sat down in the chair and positioned the rifle in the crook of my shoulder. My face was hot, and the cold, blue steel soothed me. Somewhere in the distance I heard a voice:

Yeah. He thinks he's slick. He and his bitch are trying to destroy you. Everywhere you look she's there. He stands with her at the bowling alley, not you. That's right. You know why he needed that twenty dollars? He had to give her some money. I saw them shopping. He's a fool. Don't know how to appreciate a woman like you. You're a fool, too, for putting up with his shit. Plenty of men out there will be glad to buy your groceries. Help you with those kids, too. You're the stupid one for staying here. He doesn't want you. Doesn't even need you. All he needs is a hole. Let him fuck a doughnut.

The voice began to laugh a deep, crackling, witchy sound.

Go on and do what you have to do. It'll be all right, girl. You can tell the State Troopers that your husband left you. You were home alone. You heard a noise. You went to the back door and there was a burglar. You fired in self-defense. You didn't realize it was your husband until it was too late. You didn't mean to kill him. You just didn't know it was him. They'll buy that. Besides, it'll be just another dead nigger to them, anyhow. Blow him away. Blow his head clean off.

I sat in that chair with the rifle aimed at the back door until the voice stopped talking to me. At six o'clock in the morning I got up, put the rifle away and woke up my children. Hubbie never came home that night.

I went to South Jersey and rented an apartment. I also rented a truck and drove it back to the house. By the time Hubbie arrived I had loaded everything except the refrigerator. He put that on the truck for me and helped me move our things to the apartment. I told him that I needed to be alone for a while, and we agreed that he would stay with one of his relatives.

At first it all seemed to work better. Hubbie came to the apartment on the weekends. I had begun to heal, emotionally, to the point where I was even glad to see him sometimes. But after a while his visits became more frequent. He drove a Chrysler, and gas was two dollars a gallon when he could find it. It was amazing to me that a man could live thirty minutes away from his job but couldn't find his way home, and now that he was nearly two hours away he made it "home" every night. Sometimes he would come on Friday and stay through Monday. He got in trouble on his job and they threatened to suspend him.

He really got on my nerves. I couldn't stand having him so close to me. The gurgling sound he made when he brushed his teeth drove me crazy. I was sick of him. And I was sick, period. My legs still hurt all the time, and I had an annoying ache in my lower abdomen.

I had found two lice in my pubic hair, and I went to a doctor who gave me some medicine and told me what to do. He said that my husband probably had them, too, and I should make sure he got rid of them so that I would not be re-infected. Trying to talk to Hubbie about that was almost impossible. He denied having crabs. "You probably got them from some of those white people on your job. You know how nasty they are!" But I persisted and, finally, he agreed to let me inspect him.

I could see the bugs crawling on him. I lathered him with Ivory soap and shaved his hair with a straight razor. Then I lit a candle, massaged him all over the area with the medicine, and used the tweezers to pull out the crabs. I burned sixty-two of them in the candle's flame. I stared at the razor, and then at him. For a minute I considered slicing off his dick while I had it in my hand. But he looked so pitiful, and he sounded so little boyish: "I don't want no crabs." And it occurred to me that I didn't even care enough anymore to hurt him.

The doctor had also taken a culture from my vagina. When he called a few days later to say that I had gonorrhea, I was too numb to be hurt or surprised. I went into the office and took two shots of penicillin in my ass. I didn't know very much about it, but when the doctor said it was "advanced" and asked me about Hubbie, I told him that we had not done anything for a long time. I also told him about the incident that happened six months ago:

"My husband came to me one day last September and showed me his penis. It was oozing a thick, yellow substance that looked like custard. 'I musta strained myself playing baseball,' he said. When I told him that I didn't know what to do for it and suggested that he go to a doctor he said,' I ain't going to no doctor. First thing he'll want to do is stick a finger up my ass!' So, I told him to suffer with it until it heals up."

"Well," the doctor said. "He must have gotten some help somewhere. After three days a man knows that he has the clap. He could never let it go for six months."

Like I said, I didn't care anymore. It was obvious that he didn't care about me, either. His relationship with Jessie was no longer a secret. So, the way I saw it, he had nothing to hide. If he knew he was sick six months ago and didn't think enough of me to let me know, surely he could understand that the marriage was over. Dead and stinking. All it needed was a decent burial.

I went to the shore to find him and, sure enough, I found him at the bar.

"You need to go to a doctor, " I said.

"Why?"

"It's gonorrhea."

"Oh."

I'm telling you, that's all he said. "Oh."

Next thing I know he's showing up at my apartment every single day. I couldn't hurt his feelings. I couldn't get rid of him. He started doing things he never did before. He cleaned the house, did his own laundry, put the dishes in the dishwasher and helped the kids get dressed. He only went to work when he could get gas, which was seldom. Looked like we had switched roles. I went to work and when I came home he was there with the kids. They reached a point where when they wanted to do something or go somewhere, they'd ask him, not me. I was fit to be tied.

Real estate had fallen apart, so I got a job at a bank in Philadelphia. I brought home $104 a week. Hubbie lost his job. I couldn't keep up the entire family on my salary. It was just too much.

I sent the children to stay with my mother for the summer. I put all my furniture in storage and moved in with my cousin, Joyce Ann, in the city. "What about me?" Hubbie wanted to know. In my mind I thought "What about you? Go stay with some of those folks who helped you betray me last year." But I knew that would start a fight. So, in reality I explained to him that we needed time apart, time to regroup, save some money. Get back on our feet.

"Why can't we stay together?" he said. "Always gotta be apart. I feel like I've lost everything. I lost my job. And now I've lost you."

"You didn't lose me," I said. "You threw me away."

He looked like that broke him and I thought he was going to cry. It was about time, too. I'd been doing all the crying for a long time. It was about time he showed some feelings about something. But it never happened, of course. He had this thing about being a man; real men don't show their emotions that way. So we parted that day in the same manner we usually did. Nothing was settled. He went back to Long Branch, I guess, and I went to my cousin's house in Philly.

Then something dreadful happened. Hubbie's mother died. Most of his family were ignorant of the fact that we had separated, so with a little coaxing, I went with him to the funeral to put up a front. One of his sisters did know, however, and when she offered to let me stay at her house while I was there, Hubbie latched onto my arm and said, "We travel as one." His chest was expanded, and he had a big smile.

I was the dutiful and supportive good little wife throughout the proceedings, but as soon as the funeral ended I demanded to be taken back to Philly. He dropped me off without a word.

He came back on the weekend and before I knew it he was in Philadelphia every day. Joyce Ann started to complain about having to move her children around to make room for us. She had to wash out the tub before she could get in it because he'd shower and leave his mess in the bathroom. He sat around in her way all day long while he waited for me to come home from work. It was just a mess. She'd complain about him; he'd complain about her—a woman to whom he paid no rent—and I was caught in the middle.

One of the tellers at the bank, a young Puerto Rican girl, was having trouble with her parents. We talked about her situation for weeks. She was nineteen and she dated the bank's manager. Her parents did not approve. She brought up the idea of us sharing an apartment and it sounded like a good plan. We found one in Center City Philadelphia, close to the bank. It was a high-rise building with forty stories. The swimming pool and game room were on the top floor.

Maria, her name was. She didn't have any furniture, so I took my stuff out of storage and we set up housekeeping. Hubbie didn't really understand the arrangement, but he dealt with it. I think it finally hit him that being separated meant not being together. So I had long stretches of freedom, sometimes as much as a week.

During those off days I used to sit in the lobby of the building and socialize with some of the other residents. There were lots of professional people there with interesting, stimulating conversations. Black folks, too. One young couple was about to get married and they planned a honeymoon in Europe. They were both computer programmers at IBM. Made tons of money. Then there was a white girl who illustrated children's books. There were a couple of writers, a singer, and this one guy who was an engineer. Oh, he was gorgeous. The first time I saw him he was getting on the elevator. He wore a three-piece black pin-striped suit, and as he entered the elevator he turned around and saw me just before the door closed. Almost immediately he got off the other elevator and rushed towards me saying, "I-just-want-to-know-what-is-your-name?"

I gladly gave him all my vital statistics. His name was George. The following evening when I went downstairs to loiter in the lobby, he was there waiting for me. We went to Bookbinders for dinner, and after that we became an *item*, you might say. He took me to fancy restaurants and formal, black-tie parties. I dressed up in evening gowns that he bought for me. We looked good together. Other people said so. And when it was time for us to take our relationship to another level, I invited myself to his apartment.

Indeed, this was not an easy thing for me to do. I thought about it for weeks before I did it. But I needed...*something*. I needed to feel like an attractive and desirable woman again. Then, too, if the truth be told, I needed to conquer him. I thought that would put me back in control of my life. But I was still married, and that gave me head trips about honor and decency and shit like that. Then I remembered all the things Hubbie had done to me and why I was in Philadelphia in the first place. My college roommates, and even my mother had promised that if I opened up every night I could keep him home. Yet, that had not worked. Again, I thought about Anita who once said, "What's a little piece of pussy among friends?" That line was deliciously casual, but it was powerful enough for me to base my decision on it.

He was a passionate, affectionate, gentle man. He didn't grab my breast like it was a jackhammer. He actually talked to me before, during and after. The stroke was all right--didn't measure up to my fantasies about Pop--but not bad at all, now that I think about it. He understood about my husband, and he politely stepped back whenever Hubbie just showed up.

I was living the life I had planned for me when I dreamed teenage dreams. I loved my children, but it felt good to be able to come home from work and not have to rush in and do household chores. I enjoyed an occasional nap. Mostly I appreciated the social hour downstairs in the lobby of my apartment building. People talked about travel, politics, money, music and art. My lack of education limited my input, and it fortified my determination to go back to school. I learned so much from them.

George invited me to go to Colorado for a weekend. I had never been west of Philadelphia, so I quickly accepted. We flew to Boulder on a dinner flight. I liked his friends there. The husband was a professor at the university. We picnicked on Estes mountain, shopped at a quaint little village just outside of town, and drank wine on the patio at sunset. We took lots of pictures, and I felt good. Alive. *Involved.*

I returned to my routine in Philly with new hope, but Hubbie was waiting for me in my apartment. He was fuming.

"Where the hell have you been?"

"Out."

"For three days?"

"I was out of town."

"Where?"

"Colorado."

"Who'd you go with?"

"Some of the girls at the bank. See?" I showed him some of the pictures.

He seemed to buy that and I thought I had gotten away with my lie. But he always said, "In order to be a good liar you have to have a good memory." He should know. I forgot all about the Colorado couple until they showed up three weeks later. I definitely forgot that they were in some of the pictures I had shown Hubbie. So when I introduced them to him I didn't realize that his brain was busy connecting the dots. He didn't say anything; it was his way to store information for later use.

His opportunity came about a month later when I received a letter from Mama telling me to come get my children. "I have to work," she wrote, "And it's time for them to start school."

Maria and I both knew that the apartment was too small for all of us, and since the furniture belonged to me, she decided to find herself another place. Hubbie and I drove to Wilson to pick up the kids, and when we returned, Maria was gone. That meant that she also took her half of the rent. I could not meet that rent on my pay. I couldn't buy school clothes or shoes. I could barely buy groceries. It was cold in Philadelphia and the kids didn't even have coats to wear. The finance company took back the car. And one day, I came home from work to find a padlock on my door. Hubbie and the kids were huddled together on the floor in the hallway.

I went downstairs to talk with the manager. She agreed to let me have my belongings if I would move out that very night. I called the storage company and they sent a truck to pick up my furniture. I called Solo, who lived in Willingboro, and he came with a small truck. We piled in clothes and dishes. When that truck was full, I called Ed and he let me leave some stuff in his apartment.

Of course, Hubbie was busy as worker ants getting our things together, packing stuff in boxes, taking care of his family. He made six or seven trips to George's apartment. Each time he took longer and longer to return. We finally cleared out everything and went back to Jersey where we spent the night at Solo's house.

At breakfast the next morning Solo asked me, "What y'all gonna do?"

"I don't really know, " I said. "I'm thinking about going back to North Carolina. I don't think Hubbie will follow me there. It's too far away from his family."

"Well, you don't have to leave right away. Talk to your husband. See what he has to say."

But I didn't talk to my husband. Or, rather, he didn't talk to me. He sat sulking all day, with his fists at his temples. About four o'clock in the afternoon, Solo invited me into his den. We went in and closed the door. "I don't have a whole lot of money," he said. "If I did, you know I'd help you out. I don't know what kind of man that is you got in there, but he worries me. He don't even talk. I'm afraid he'll hurt you."

"Oh, don't worry about Hubbie," I told him. He's harmless. He just acts the fool once in a while, that's all."

"I don't think the man is acting."

Solo had some reefer and he offered me a drag. I'd tried it before but it did nothing for me. Didn't know how to do it I guess. So, when I declined, he insisted. "Come on. This is some good shit. It'll help you think better. Just try it." I took the joint and let him coach me. I took a long drag and held it deep in my lungs. Then I took another. And another. In a little while everything just sort of mellowed out. All the things that were bothering me didn't seem to matter anymore. I felt good. Relaxed. I even laughed a little. After what seemed like days later Solo said that my husband was really angry. I heard myself say, "I don't give a fuck."

I emerged from that room with a plan. I would tell Hubbie that I didn't want to be married anymore. I would take the children and move back to Wilson, get myself a job, go back to school and get on with my life. Hubbie took one look at me and he spoke first.

"You don't need to smoke that shit. You look terrible."

"Why are you picking on me?"

"Oh, you're paranoid now, huh?"

"I have something to tell you."

"Good, 'cause I'm ready to hear it. Come on in here and let's talk about it." He grabbed my arm and led me to the bedroom. "Maybe now that you got your courage up, you can tell the truth for a change."

He pushed me down on the bed and when I sat up, he sat on the floor between my knees. "Didn't you tell me that you went to Colorado with a bunch of girls?"

"Yes. So?"

"Well how did your little engineer friend get copies of those pictures?"

"What did you do, rummage through the man's apartment?"

"Naw, I didn't have to do that. He had them sitting right there on the coffee table. I think I saw him in one of them, too."

"What are you accusing me of, Hubbie?"

"Did you go to Colorado with him?"

I thought about lying again. Then I thought about Jessie. I wanted to hurt him as much as he had hurt me.

"Yes."

"Did you go to bed with him?"

"Yes."

"How many times?"

"What?"

"How many times?"

"What difference does that make?"

"When you found out about Jessie, didn't I tell you that it was only one time?"

That pissed me off. I raised my voice, which wasn't smart, and I attacked him directly. "No, you did not tell me that! You can't possibly expect me to be stupid enough to believe some dumb shit like that anyway. You spent two years with her. Two whole years. Everybody thought *she* was your wife. I worked my ass off while you were laid up with that outdoor strumpet! What, are you keeping score now?"

Of course, that was the wrong thing to say. All of a sudden I saw lightning and I felt thunder. It took a moment for my brain to register that Hubbie was beating me with his fists on my face and head. It looked like he never would stop. When my mind realized that he was going to kill me, I couldn't do anything but grab him around his waist and hold on. I screamed, "Oh God!" And he said, "God can't help you now. God ain't got time for a trashy bitch like you. Call on the devil, 'cause your ass is going to hell."

He stopped hitting me then and went over to the closet. He searched frantically for something on the shelf. I knew he was looking for his gun, but I sat there, silent, listening to my flesh swell. My eye popped and crackled and sounded like plastic wrap unraveling. Unable to find what he was looking for, he began to pace the floor. And the noise that was coming out of him: "Fuckin' bitch! Fuckin' filthy bitch! Spite pussy!"

Solo rushed into the room with a .357magnum in his hand. "What the fuck is going on in here?"

"Ask your cousin," Hubbie said. Then he yanked my arm and dragged me into the living room where my children were huddled together on the sofa. "Tell them! Tell them why I did it!"

"Hubbie...don't ...I didn't do that to you."

Everybody talked at one time then. *Mommy...your face...hospital... no...get out of the way...doctor...help me...no hospital... Mommy, Mommy, look at your face.*

I pulled away from Hubbie and went back into the bedroom. He followed me. I tried to get my coat. "Where do you think you're going?" he said.

"Solo's going to take me to the hospital."

"You don't need no hospital. You'll be all right. Look. I'm sorry. I don't know what happened. Everything just went black. I didn't mean it."

"Whether you meant it or not, I'm still just as beat up."

"You made me do it. I love you. I'd never do anything to hurt you."

"If you love me so much, you need to let Solo take me to the hospital."

"I said no. No hospital. First thing they'll want to know is who did this to you. Then I have to go to jail. You don't want that. Do you...baby?"

At that moment all I wanted was to get out of that room. But he held me close, cooing soft words of apology, until we both fell asleep.

I awoke before dawn the next morning and went into the bathroom.

The sight of my face in the mirror horrified me. There were huge lumps in my head. My lip was busted and so fat that I couldn't tell where the lip ended and the chin began. The top part of my eye was swollen shut, and the skin underneath sagged onto my cheek. The whole side of my face had shifted. It looked like I'd had a stroke. It was deep purple and sticky with old blood.

I AM TWENTY-NINE YEARS OLD. Married, with two kids. *I know what this is. It is all too familiar. I am a student of my own history. Mama beaten. Grandma Easter beaten to death. My friend Barbara Booker Pitts stabbed to death . Barbara Jean Leach beaten to death with a shovel. So much violence against women…all at the hands of men who are supposed to love and protect them. I dream about snakes. I sleep with my enemy. I dream about guns. My husband wants to kill me. He says I am going to hell. Compared to this, I think it would be a vacation.*

I stare at myself in this mirror. I am in the same shape as my mother. I don't want to be married to him anymore, and at least, now I know why. I am afraid of him. I am scared to leave him again, and I am afraid to stay with him. I don't know what to do. It isn't about love. I have never loved him in a way that I cannot let him go. But there was a time when I respected him. Now that is gone, and with it went my innocence. That is the hard part. My little Sunday school, fairy tale ideas about living happily ever after are destroyed. There is no hope. No fantasy of some brave and handsome prince riding through on his big white horse to rescue me. None. I am in a mess and I cannot see my way out of it. I have two children I can't feed, let alone give them a place to stay.

I have the nerve to think about going to college. The first and last thing on my mind every day is college. I think about it now. The thought is the only thing that keeps me from slashing my wrist in this bathroom. I'll go back to college and get myself out of this mess. Things can get better for us. People who have college degrees talk through their problems instead of fighting all the time. Hubbie is stronger, sure enough. But I am smart. It might take some time, but I can figure out a way to go to school and make him think it is his idea.

In the meantime, I'll make him think he is right. I deserved that beating. I provoked him. I can make him think that I am willing to surrender. I'll be a good wife again.

twelve

I apologized to Solo for bringing my troubles into his home. We left that morning and went to the train station. The plan was to start over. We had to wait at the station five hours before the train departed, and during that time we made a vow that no other outsiders would come between us ever again. I promised not to work.

We arrived in Wilson at ten in the morning. My father and mother were appalled at the sight of my face. Mama said, "These things happen in a marriage." And after a brief interview with Hubbie, my father said, "You just like yo' mammy. Better keep yo' ass in check, girl. Make yo' husband happy so this don't happen no mo'. Ya hear?"

My shame made me stay close to home. I didn't want to see any of my old girlfriends who, naturally, wanted to meet my family. I'd send my sister to the door to tell them that I was busy or asleep or gone. The only time I left the house was when Hubbie had something to do downtown, like get a haircut or go to the gun shop. Then he'd parade me through my hometown like I was a trophy of some sort, showing off my eye. It took a long time to heal, and I wore a beret pulled way down on the side to hide it. I was very self-conscious about it. People stared at me, and they condemned him with their eyes. At one point Hubbie looked at me and said, " Look at that. That's a shame." As if someone else had done it.

Hubbie found a job within days of our arrival, and my mother was as busy as she could be trying to find one for me. I tried to explain that Hubbie didn't want me to work, but she insisted that I get a job so that we could move out of her house. That made sense. He and Mama did not get along. She accused him of being lazy. He was. He accused her of being mouthy. She was. What he called 'nosy,' she called 'community concern.' I was caught in the middle because though neither of them talked to each other, they each talked about the other to me. The tension gave me headaches. Hubbie wanted to fuck all the time and I couldn't bring myself to do it in my mother's house. That made him mad. He'd sit around the house with his arms folded and his mouth clamped shut. Wouldn't even talk to the kids when he was like that.

I was trapped again. Every time Mama got a chance she'd tell me, "You ain't got *nothing* for a husband." That made me angry. I knew he wasn't shit. Hell, he knew he wasn't shit. The last thing I needed was for my mother to tell me he wasn't shit. They kept me so nervous I couldn't even think. I lost a lot of weight—went down to a hundred and seven pounds. Just about time I thought I would have a stroke and die, Mama found me a job as a secretary at my old elementary school.

As fortune reverts to misfortune, Hubbie was laid off just before Christmas. Our stay at Mama's house had to be extended. But early in the spring he got a job at a tire and rubber company and we moved into a house in the suburbs of Wilson. We drove to Philadelphia on a weekend and picked up our things.

Hubbie made four times my salary. Nothing would satisfy me but to gain employment where he worked. I figured that since I had to work eight hours a day anyway, I might as well make as much money as I could and save some for college. Besides, I wasn't doing well on my job at Sam Vick Elementary. Just wasn't the secretary type. I didn't mind taking orders from Mr. Dixon, the principal, but I refused to take orders from the teachers and their aides. One of the unspoken, unwritten duties I was expected to perform was to make coffee every morning. Since it was not in my job description, I would not do it. That caused some confusion and rather heated discussions. So the librarian made the coffee every morning and I acquired the title *feminist.* The way they curled down their mouths when they said *feminist* made it sound like a dirty word. I could hear them whispering about how I thought I was too cute to make the principal's coffee.

They just didn't get it. It wasn't about a lousy cup of coffee. It was the principle of it. If I had offered, that would be one thing, but to try to make a servant out of me was something else again. Suppose he had a male secretary. All the women in that office would fall all over each other trying to be first to make coffee. They don't even realize that they are the reason women have so much trouble on the job front. They switch into that office with their breasts jiggling, and serve up coffee, when what they are really trying to do is get in tight with the boss. I read a book one time, *Houseboy* was the name of it, which said, "The dog of the king is the king of the dogs." And once you become king (or in this case, queen), of the dogs, you can get away with some really bizarre shit. And you can control all the other dogs. Next thing you know, he slaps one of them on the ass with a newspaper. She giggles and lets him get away with it. She's in now, see. So, he figures he can do it to everybody. Then when someone like me comes along and mentions a phrase like *sexual harassment,* the women turn on the women because he's just trying to be friendly. See how that works?

But enough of that. I digress. The important thing is that I did get a job at the rubber company, and I gave my notice and got out of Sam Vick.

Within a year, Hubbie and I had saved enough money to make a down payment on our own house. Notice that I did not call it a *home.* That's because it didn't feel like home to me. It was simply a place to be. An address. A place where I could choose whether or not to follow the rules that somebody else had set for me. By now you should know well the nature of my spirit. I'm talking about rules that are particularly governed by time. Six o'clock in the morning, time to eat breakfast. Eight o'clock, time to take the kids to school. Twelve noon, time for lunch. Four o'clock, time to pick up the kids. Six in the evening, time for dinner. Eight o'clock, time to put the kids to bed. Eleven at night…humph! We're married…you know what time that is.

Think about that for a minute. Everything we do involves following or breaking rules. Like what I'm doing right now when I speak to you, the reader, directly. I know I am supposed to tell you some nice things about Hubbie so you can like him. I should make him a *credible character.* But what I am telling you is the truth and I couldn't care less whether you like him or not. I've tried to tell this story before, but I dropped the notion because I am smart enough now to realize that I allowed that to happen. It is difficult to communicate with a man who speaks with his hands and feet, and I really didn't want you to know about it at first because it no longer defines me. You'd probably say, "Why doesn't she just leave?" And it is not as simple as that because I thought I was tough; I was strong, and I did not want you to measure me by the number of ass-whippings I could take.

Every once in a while I'd break a rule or two, especially that last one. Hubbie didn't beat me every day, oh no, nothing like that. But he'd say things that made me feel like I'd been whipped. He always gave very practical gifts: a washing machine, a vacuum cleaner, a new set of cookware. Anniversaries or Valentine's Day were just normal days to him. Sometimes he'd be at home, sometimes he wouldn't. While I envied the other women at work whose men sent them chocolates and flowers, Hubbie reasoned: "Candy makes you fat, and flowers remind me of dead people." And then one day, I told him that a guy at work had said that I was beautiful. The comment lifted my spirits, but my husband said, "You let them white people tell you anything, don't you? Now, I'll admit that you're cute. But *beautiful?* C'mon, Barbara, you can look in the mirror."

That hurt. Most women carry these thoughts with them, even into the bedroom. I was no different. And when I did not want to perform that chore, well, hell, there was another fight. For the life of me I couldn't figure out which was worse, having Hubbie scream, "What's the matter? Don't you fuck no more?" or surrendering out of a sense of duty to loveless, violent and painful sex.

Either way, I was beaten. Hubbie started his same old routine of staying out late at night. So you tell me…if a man doesn't drink, gamble, smoke or do drugs, what's left to keep him out until three in the morning in a town that goes to sleep at nine?

He took me for a ride one day and he pointed out all the whorehouses in Wilson. After Grandma Easter died I did not know such places existed. Then he came home one day and told me all about this woman at work who had confided in him. He said her husband had treated her really bad. Wouldn't come home at night. Didn't buy anything for the kids at Christmas. Didn't spend New Year's Eve with her. Hubbie said he felt sorry for her. Ha! He felt sorry for her. He didn't feel sorry for me when he did the same thing. And thinking about that put me right back into the miserable frame of mind I was trying so hard to escape.

I can see now that I overcompensated for my misery by buying things. I bought fancy things that I didn't need and really didn't even want once I got them. Televisions sets, top of the line computerized sewing machines, motorcycles for everybody in the family. And though I say, "I," it was "we." Hubbie would help me buy anything I wanted because it made him look good. So everyone thought we were happy because we worked together, put our money together and bought things. They saw him as a good provider because he put me in that fine house. He bought me that customized van. He saw to it that the kids and I dressed very well. I always had money to spend. And he even touched me in public.

That caused a lot of resentment on my part, I'll admit. I was the one who bought clothes for the family. I picked out the van. I talked with the builder and set up the contract to buy the fine house. Even my father said, "How's he goin' to put somebody in something' when everybody's workin'?" And about the "touching in public" part…whenever he locked arms with me as we walked somewhere, it wasn't about affection; it was about control.

I kept my mouth shut and let Hubbie take all the credit. Needless to say, when I finally left him, I became the pariah of Wilson. Folks just couldn't understand how I could leave such a good man. Now, I'm going to tell you how that happened, but, as they say in poker, this is where it gets down and dirty.

thirteen

The best lesson I have ever learned in life is how to look at myself from the inside out. Sometimes things happen that might appear to be wrong on the surface, but when you re-examine them in hindsight, you realize that they were exactly right. So when I did what I did, I thought it was wrong. Evil and wicked. Bad. Perhaps that's what made it so deliciously good.

I had started my new job as a trainee. At the time I was the only woman in our department. My instructor was a man about five years younger than I. He was cute. He had a juicy and full bottom lip and a smile that flashed a whole set of pearls. He was polite and caring, and he called me "Lady." He taught me how to do the work and then he'd leave me alone to let me do it. Didn't hang over me all the time, but trusted me to do it properly. His name was Ronald, and even though I didn't see him spying on me, whenever I ran into trouble he'd magically appear without being summoned.

I was attracted to him from the beginning and I knew it. It was mutual, and I knew that, too. Only problem was, we didn't have the right to do anything about it. So we kept lying to ourselves and each other, trying to pretend that our friendship came out of our working relationship.

He was a very gentle and attentive man. If I wore my hair a different way he'd notice and comment on it. He'd say things like, "Lady, what's that perfume you're wearing?" or, "I like that shirt, Lady. Peach looks good on you." And one time, when I got gas in my eye, he put his hand on my shoulder and led me to the washroom.

He should have never done that. His touch made me quiver with desire. What I should have done was figure out a way to lay him right then. In that way it would have been a simple affair. Would have been over. I could have gone back to my life of pretense and nobody would have to know. Life can be so easy when you keep things on a physical level. Emotions complicate shit.

But as it turned out, I waited for over a year. By that time I was sure that I was in love with him, and for the first time in my life since Pop, I could feel my love being returned. He was supportive and complimentary, and the gleam in his eye when he looked at me was beyond compare. He made love to my mind; he dominated my thoughts. So when the telephone would ring at home and Hubbie said it was a wrong number, I did not care that he had to suddenly go to the store.

At the end of my training we went into a conference room to discuss my progress. It was close in that room and I could not concentrate on what he said. I kept thinking about how good it would feel to drag him to the floor and wrap my thighs around his back. I found myself telling him all about Hubbie and Jessie. I don't know why I did that. I must have been trying to show him that my marriage was not as perfect as everybody seemed to think. I might have been trying to tell him that his caring nature was what I needed. Hell, I could have been trying to show him that I was available for play. I just don't know. But he didn't bite. He said, "Well, y'all came out of it together. That's what's important."

So, I didn't tell him what was on my mind. Instead, I substituted him in my bedroom and gave Hubbie all the lust I had for Ronald. I'd shut my eyes real tight and fantacize Ronald. But whenever I opened my eyes, Hubbie was always there. That made me feel dirty, dishonest. Hubbie thought our marriage was back on solid ground. It didn't stop him from staying out late at night when he wanted to, but he expected me to understand that he was a man.

Then one day Ronald came to my machine and said, "Lady, I found a woman just like you. I think I'm going to marry her."

My God. That just about killed me. I offered him my congratulations, but I could almost hear my heart breaking into little pieces.

"I want you to meet her," he said.

"Why?"

"Because I need your approval. If there's anything wrong with her I can trust you to let me know."

I made arrangements for them to come to dinner. She was young, pretty and ambitious. She called me "Ma'am," and aside from that I honestly couldn't find anything wrong with her. The only thing I wanted for him or from him was his complete happiness. If he was lucky enough to find that, my little feelings did not matter at all. So I gave him the thumbs up and he married her the following month around Thanksgiving.

I didn't go to the wedding. Couldn't. Hubbie and I took the kids down to South of the Border and spent the entire weekend. He asked me about it, Hubbie did:

"What's the matter?"

"Nothing."

"Why do you look so sad?"

"I'm just tired, that's all."

"Did you want to go to the wedding?"

"No."

"Then what's the matter?"

"Nothing."

Ronald and his wife were married for three weeks before they separated. I don't know what happened. Don't care to know. I do know that he was absolutely miserable after the first week. There was a dullness in his eyes, and the mouth full of pearls was clamped shut all the time. Everyone at our lunch table crowd noticed the change in him. One of the guys tried to joke:

"Say, Ron. How's that wife of yourn?"

"She's aw-ite."

"I been meaning to tell ya….if it was a wife ya wanted ya coulda had that one I got."

We all laughed at that and Ronald seemed to loosen up a little bit. So the guy kept going: "Ya oughta be a happy man. Ya doubled yo' income."

I remembered how little money I had made at Sam Vick. I said, "He hasn't doubled his income. She works in the school system and makes minimum wage. If anything, she's tripled hers."

"Well I shoulda knowed that you'd take up for him. Let you tell it, he can't do no wrong."

The whole world stood still right then. Everybody in the cafeteria looked dead at me. I felt my face get hot. I thought I had been so careful with my secret. I politely excused myself and got up to leave. As I walked away from the table I heard the guy say to Ronald, "You bangin' that, ain't ya?" And he said, "No."

It was the God's truth. But, see, that's something you can never deny. If you say no, they don't believe you because that's what you're supposed to say. If you say 'yes' their response will be "See? I knew it!" But then you really would be lying. It's one of those lose/lose situations.

Then, too, I didn't like the way the guy referred to me as a *that*. Like I was a piece of furniture or something. Ronald was not even about that. He treated me with respect. I didn't have to see his face to know that he didn't like what the guy had said about me. And that made me want him even

73

more. So when he came to my machine later that day, I asked him to meet me somewhere and he said, "Okay."

I could give you all the details, but I won't. I will tell you, however, that he took me to places within myself that I had never known. With him I felt like I was a book, and he read every single page. All of the *do this…or let's try that…*wasn't necessary. The boy knew what to do. You'd think that a woman's body was his own invention, and I had no clue what was happening until it happened.

I used to stand at my machine and cry, thinking about the way my life had turned. Ronald put an end to all that. Being with him gave me hope and meaning. He gave me a reason to get up every day. He made me forget all about my fantasies about Pop, and that took some doing. Whenever I'd see him I'd break out in a broad grin. So did he. Once he said, "You know, they say that people who are in love smile a lot."

I became extremely tolerant of Hubbie. The things he did didn't bother me anymore. It was not a big deal that he'd stay out late; I'd go to sleep and save my energy for Ronald. On the few occasions that Hubbie and I did get together, I knew that we were both substitutes.

It wasn't long before I realized that I couldn't keep up at the rate I was going. I wanted to leave Hubbie for good. I didn't want to leave him for Ronald; I wanted to leave for myself. I saw my happiness as an entitlement, and I wanted to be free to enjoy the goodness life had to offer.

Hubbie would never let me go unless he was involved with someone. He had girlfriends, I knew. I could always tell when he was with one of them because there would be an unexplained withdrawal of fifty dollars from our bank account. But he did not have a stable outside relationship like the one with Jessie. He came home one night and the spoiler was missing from the van. He told me that he ran into a huge puddle of water on the golf course and broke it. Hell, Hubbie didn't play golf. So, even though I knew in my heart that he was seeing someone, I had not "caught" him at it. Didn't have any proof. So, I kept putting off the inevitable.

But life has a funny way of forcing an issue. A lot of my cousins were in town to celebrate Grandma Josephine's ninetieth birthday. We all decided to go to a club, and since Hubbie did not like nightclubbing, I was allowed to go alone with my relatives. I called Ronald and arranged for him to be there. At the end of the night, I went home with him.

He and his wife were still separated and were planning a divorce. But Ronald had been injured in a motorcycle accident a week earlier, and he let her come to see him. It hurt like hell, but what could I do? I was married, too. What difference did it make anyway? His wife, my husband…neither of them could begin to understand what we felt for each other.

So, we did what we both wanted to do and we lay in each other's arms talking about our hopeless situation. We never heard the car drive up, never heard the door slam. She came into the house and talked briefly with Ronald's uncle (he had moved back to the homestead). Her voice was loud. Too loud. It disturbed my peace. Ronald immediately put on his pants and covered me with a blanket.

"Who is that?" I asked him.

"It's my wife."

Before I had time to panic, she kicked in the door of our room and strolled in.

I will never forget the hurt on her face. Oh, she was angry, no doubt about that. But that woman was hurt. She reminded me of myself so many years ago. Even today that look haunts my memory, and I promised myself that night that I would never again be involved with a married man. I have been on both sides of that revelation, and neither of them is comfortable.

"What is this shit?" she said, and it looked like she was directing her question at me.

"I love him," I said.

"I can see that, but what is this shit?"

"What are you doing here?" Ronald wanted to know.

"I asked you, 'What is this shit?'"

"And I asked you what you're doing here?"

"The same thing I was doing here last night."

"I know about that," I said.

"And the night before?"

"I know about that, too."

"Well, you must be some kind of new fool, then."

"Maybe. But I love him, and I won't give him up."

"I think you should leave. I need to talk to him."

"Fine with me. You mind waiting outside while I get dressed?"

"Not at all."

She stepped out of the room. Ronald turned to me and said, "Baby, I'm sorry."

"It's not your fault," I said. "But I do have to tell Hubbie. You know that, right?"

He knew, but I don't think either of us was prepared for Hubbie's reaction.

I went straight home and woke up Hubbie. There must have been something on my face because he sat up in the bed and gave me his full attention. I was scared half to death. This really was a reason for him to kill me. But I braced myself for whatever was going to happen, and I tried to prepare him, too.

"I have something to tell you. It's going to hurt really bad."

I told him the whole story. Knowing him the way I thought I did, I could have never anticipated his question:

"Why didn't you go out of town, or something? So nobody would know."

He reached for me and I started to run, but then I realized that he wanted to hug me. He said, "I'm not going to hurt you. I love you. And I understand. I knew somebody was in this bed with us."

I didn't know what to do with that. It just wasn't the Hubbie I knew. I expected at least a punch in the mouth. But nothing. He held me until the sun came up, and he assured me that everything would be all right.

At ten o'clock that morning the phone rang and Hubbie answered it. It was Ronald. They arranged to meet. To *talk*. I wanted to go, but Hubbie said this was a "man" thing. "Don't worry," he said. "We're just going to talk. But before I go, I need to know how you feel about him."

He did not ask me how I felt about *him*. He owned me, so I think he assumed that he knew. So when I said, "I care a lot about him," I think Hubbie thought there was hope for us because I did not use the word *love*.

That was my biggest mistake. I should have told him right then that I loved Ronald. It would have been finished. But I didn't have the nerve standing there in his face like that. So I let him think that Ronald was a *problem* that we would have to work out when, in fact, Ronald had become my whole world.

When the men met for their talk, I went to see Ronald's wife. Women do go after each other in times like this, and I didn't want her to come to my house and start some shit in front of my children. I had gone to see Jessie, and it got nasty. But I was fully armed with my .25 at the time, and that gave me courage to tell her all about her ancestors. Now that I am older and wiser, I wonder why we do things like that. We women attack each other and challenge each other to a duel, when the man is the one who has the obligation to us. He is the one who betrays us. Why don't we go after him? It's funny to me now, but we make him the prize, and we fight each other tooth and nail until one of us surrenders. Or dies. He keeps us in competition and we subscribe to it. In doing that we co-sign his sense of superiority. If the wife fails to do something that the outside woman does, or vice versa, it gives him license to do whatever he chooses. He can point his finger and tell her it is all her fault. Then she breaks her back trying to be like the other woman, or trying to get rid of her, thinking that if she succeeds, he will be exclusively hers. By the end of the battle, more often than not, he's already found another ally and the cycle starts all over again.

Ronald's wife was talking on the phone with her sister when I got there. She told me to "Come on in." It was a little awkward for a minute, with me standing in her living room while she finished her conversation. After a while, though, she hung up the phone and asked me why I was there.

"I thought we needed to talk—"

"About what?"

"About last night. I didn't mean—"

"It doesn't matter what you meant."

"I didn't mean to hurt you. I thought your marriage was over, and—"

"'Thought' thought he farted, but guess what? Big old lump of shit in his pants."

"Look—"

"No, you look. What was on your mind? You got everything a woman could want. Half the women in this town envy you. Look around you." She waved her hand to show off her house. Nice. Black leather furniture. Red pillows. Black and white curtains. "It ain't much, I admit. But it's mine. I bought it. I paid for it. That empty spot over there? That's where the television was that he bought for my birthday. When he left, he took it with him. Said I didn't deserve a TV. I got nothing. You hear me? Nothing."

"I thought you wanted it that way. Thought you guys were getting a divorce."

"There the papers sit. Right there. But he won't sign 'em."

"Why?"

"You tell me."

"I don't have any answers for you."

"Then why did you come?"

"I just wanted you to know that I wasn't trying to take anything from you. It wasn't …cheap. I love him."

"Yeah…that's what he said about you. Humph! Two fools together. I don't know what's the matter with you. You got a good husband. A good husband. That man loves the hell out of you."

"How do you know?"

I did not get an answer to that question because Hubbie drove up. I did not ask him how he knew where she lived, either. But he opened her door and walked in as if he paid the rent there. It was an intrusion. An invasion. I wasn't allowed to go with him to talk with Ronald, but here he was in my conversation with her. I left. I could take anything she could dish out, one on one, but I was not about to let them double team me. Besides, they were both victims now, and I already knew what they would discuss: *She did this and he did that so why don't we get together and do something?*

Hubbie came into the house right behind me. "Ronald said he loves you."

"I know. What did you say?"

"Told him I couldn't blame him for that. I love you, too."

He looked so pitiful right then. I was sorry. I put my arms around him and held him for a long time. Now. I have to admit that I was not sorry for what I did. I was sorry that it went down the way it did. Sorry that I had caused so much pain just because I loved somebody. And I was sorry that everyone would know. Wilson is a small town that feeds on gossip and other people's heartache. What made it so bad, Hubbie, Ronald and I all worked at the same place and on the same shift. Ronald's wife spent the entire weekend on the phone, telling everyone she knew what the "low-life mother fucker and his bitch" had done to her. By the time we got to work the place was all a-buzz with the news about our little triangle. Folks who had never spoken a word to me actually got up in my face to ask me if it was true. They did the same thing with Ronald and with Hubbie, and that's when the real Hubbie came back: "You see the kind of humiliation I have to suffer just because you wanted to fuck somebody?"

Ronald and I went out of our way to avoid each other at work. I guess we both knew that all eyes were on us. But we also knew we had to talk about this. We decided to meet in the woods out by Wilson Lake.

I signed the divorce papers," he said.

"I figured you would after all this."

"What are you going to do?"

"I don't know."

"I want you to come stay with me."

"I can't."

"Why not?"

"I have to think about the kids. I don't know what I'm going to do, but I have to think about them."

"You can bring them, too. I can take care of you. All of you."

It sounded too good to be true. I didn't think I deserved to have the love of this kind of man. I had to think hard about my children and what a divorce could do to them. What about Mama? She and Ronald's mother went to the same church. They would both be so embarrassed if we "shacked up." And what about Hubbie? If I left him he could divorce me on the grounds of desertion. I didn't want that cloud hanging over my head when I stood at the pearly gates.

What I really wanted, I think, was for Hubbie to put me out. That way, the decision would be his. Then I could take the comfortable role of victim. But he wouldn't do that, I was sure of it. I also knew that he would never leave me, and that put me in a kind of standstill like a sea crab. I could move from side to side, but I couldn't go forward, and I refused to go backward. What if I did leave Hubbie for Ronald? Would the love stop when the ownership began? I was confused, and I needed more time.

"Hubbie loves me," I said.

"And you love him."

"No. I love you."

"You *care* about me. He told me that you said so."

He seemed angry then. I started to say something but he covered my mouth with his. "I'll wait," he said. "For as long as it takes."

I AM THIRTY-TWO YEARS OLD. *I wish I could tell you how much I ache. I just don't have the words. It is like being on a broken down elevator. Stuck between two floors. If I take a chance, I can climb out, but I might slip and fall. Plunge to my death. If I stay put, depending on someone else to rescue me, I could suffocate. I have no one I can trust to help me. I can't talk to anyone about this. My family has deserted me, especially my mother and father. The scandal is too much for them to handle. I feel dizzy with apprehension all the time. I keep expecting something drastic to happen. In everything I do I am only half there. I don't eat. I drink beer for breakfast. I have lost a lot of weight.*

I am sick all the time. Kidney infections keep me weak and feverish. As soon as I get rid of one, here comes another. I spend much of my shift in the infirmary at work. I miss too many days and the boss threatens to fire me.

My husband is beyond angry, beyond mad. Furious is a good word to describe him. He is furious at me all the time. Nothing I do satisfies him. He has an excuse now—or perhaps a reason—to abuse me. It looks like his entire mission in life is to make me as miserable as he can.

Tonight I feel unusually tired. I drink a lot of coffee and I swallow some honey, trying to stay awake. At the eight o'clock dinner break I take two No Doze tablets. They give me a terrible headache. At nine-thirty I take two Excedrin. I am really nervous. My hands and legs shake really bad. At ten o'clock I feel a rush of heat all over and everything goes black. I pass out. When I regain consciousness I am stretched out on the floor screaming. My whole body shakes. I cannot see. I hear voices. A lot of them. Someone shouts, "Go get Hubbie! Go get Hubbie!" Gradually my sight comes back. The first thing I see is Hubbie standing over me with his arms folded across his chest. Two guys lift me onto a stretcher.

I am in the ambulance on my way to the hospital. By the time I get there I am no longer shaking. The doctor says I have "anxiety," and he gives me valium to take. He says I should avoid anything with caffeine in it. The diagnosis is not good enough for my husband. Maybe I should die or something. He says, "Anxiety, huh? I'd be too shamed to tell it. If I had known that's all it was I would have stayed the fuck at work."

I wonder how other women fare in times like this. Their husbands seem to care about their health. Not mine. Ever. My illnesses are inconveniences to him.

fourteen

Taking valium kept me dazed. Slowed-down. But I wasn't getting any better; the kidney infections kept coming. Finally, my doctor advised me that the neck of my bladder was too small to pass the bacteria. It would have to be enlarged. He suggested an in-office operation that would take about half an hour. I agreed to do it because he made it sound so simple.

But I wasn't ready for what actually happened. That half hour seemed like an eternity. Doctor had to get to my bladder through my vagina. He couldn't use an anesthetic, he said. He used a long instrument that looked like a knitting needle, and on the end of it was the tiniest pair of scissors. It hurt so bad...it didn't hurt. I winced with the first little snip and moved my hips away from him. The doctor yelled at me and warned that if I moved again he might puncture my bladder and I could die right there on the table. So, I dug my nails into my palms and let him do his work. When he finished, the insides of my hands were bloody.

The doctor told me that I should not have sex for six weeks. That was a relief to me, but when I told Hubbie about it he said, "I'm tired of you being sick! I can't never get no pussy!"

I think that is when I first began to realize that pussy was about all I meant to him. A convenient, in-house, free pussy. He'd never approached sex in a romantic way. "Gimme some" was about as close as he came. I never *wanted* to do it anymore, and after that, whenever I saw him coming with his dick in his hand, I'd just roll over on my side and let him have his way. But I did tell him one time, "You know, if I ever stop trying in this marriage, it will fall apart." I read a poem one time by Yeats. It said something like: "Things fall apart when the center cannot hold." I saw myself as the center, and I could not hold on much longer.

fifteen

By now you must be sick of reading about this long saga of my bondage. So, I will get quickly to the point of how and why I finally left Hubbie. Since I was not an active participant in the bedroom, he found other ways to satisfy his sexual appetite. Most of them were familiar. Women would call the house or they'd have some man call. Our phone number was unlisted, but they asked for him by name. If I was standing nearby, he'd say, "You got the wrong number." And, of course, after he hung up the phone he'd have to go to the store or go get gas or something. It didn't bother me one little bit. I wanted him to find somebody. He was gone practically every night and I was eating better, sleeping better, finding my way back to health.

One night I had a dream, I thought. I was drowning, smothering in some thick gooey substance like quicksand. It was in my mouth and eyes. It found its way up my nose. I tried to wipe it away, and in the process, I woke up. Hubbie was kneeling over me. I was too horrified to speak. "I'm sorry," he said. "You just looked so pretty in the moonlight."

This one thing, the proverbial straw, made me give up on Hubbie completely. If he could do that to me in my sleep, he could just as easily cut my throat. It was either complete hatred for me or perversion that made him do a thing like that. Either way, I was a dead woman if I stayed there. Whether it was dead and in the ground, or dead by simply not living, didn't matter anymore. It was all the same, except the first one was an escape to freedom; the second one was a condemnation to hell.

A whole year had passed since my involvement with Ronald. I had given this marriage all I had. I felt cheated out of the love of my life because I was married to Hubbie. But it wasn't about Ronald anymore. It was about me. I wanted to be the one who decided who I could and could not love. I wanted to be the captain of my fate, the conqueror of my soul. I wanted to have the responsibility for my own life.

I sat myself down and did a little Barbara inventory. I didn't fit in this scene. I was Hubbie's wife, my kids' mother, Mama's and Daddy's daughter, my sister's sister, somebody's friend, somebody's niece, somebody's cousin in every aspect of my life. But where was I? I had given out so many pieces of myself that there was hardly any me left. I believed I was born for a reason. A purpose. That purpose was not clear to me, but it was bigger than I was. Bigger than Hubbie. Bigger, even, than Wilson. Changes had to be made in the world and I was the one chosen to do it. I had to get out of that marriage so the world could continue.

Jerry Butler and Brenda Lee Edgar had recorded a song that didn't even rhyme, but it was a hit because it made so much sense. The name of it was *Ain't Understanding Mellow?* In that song, the man compliments the woman for letting him know that their relationship is all wrong. They part with respect for each other. I must have played that song a hundred times during the next week. It gave me courage to leave.

At the end of the week I sat Hubbie down on the edge of the bed and told him what was on my mind. I knew he was seeing one of my distant cousins, but his response was a surprise to me. He let me go. But he said something very important to me that day. Maybe he was trying to show me that I was dependent on him for my survival. Maybe he was trying to prove it to himself. I don't know...but on that day, when I told him that I did not want to be married anymore, he said, "I can promise you one thing: Your life will be very different without me!"

He had no idea how much I was counting on that to be true. The way I saw it, if I got out there and *fell* on my face, at least I'd have the satisfaction of knowing that I fell and nobody pushed me.

I packed a few of my work clothes and went to stay with my mother. I took nothing else. Didn't want anything else. He could have the house, the cars and the furniture. I was happy to escape with my life. I even left my children. But when Monday rolled around I realized that I had left my make-up case at his house, and Barbara doesn't go anywhere without eyebrows.

I took some groceries for him and the kids. He accused me of running back and forth. I certainly didn't want to cramp his style, so I never went back after that.

I found an apartment and my older daughter came to live with me. The little one was ten, and she wanted to stay with her father because "somebody has to take care of Daddy." But when Hubbie and his girlfriend and another couple went to the movies one night and left her all alone in the house, she called everywhere looking for me. He grabbed me by the arm at work the next day and said, "I think it is a damned shame when a ten year-old girl can't find her mother at night."

"Where were you?"

"I have a right to a life! You know I can't stand to be alone. I can't be there to watch her every minute. You're her mother. You're supposed to take care of her."

"Okay…I'll come get her."

"Whaddaya mean you'll come get her? She's lonely, Barbara. She needs to have her family back together. You deserted me. That's what you did. All you did was split up the money. I'm not happy. You come home and make me happy!"

"I can't do that. But I will talk with her and see what she wants to do. If she wants to come live with me she's welcome."

"Well don't you think you need to do something legal about this?"

"Like what?"

"I need you to get a legal separation!"

"Why?"

"For the same reason you're gonna need it eventually. I need somebody to go to bed with, that's why!"

"What about your friend?"

"Aw…she won't do nothing 'cause she thinks you're gonna come back."

"Tell her not to worry."

I picked up my child from school that day and we had a long talk. She cried, and that was really hard on me. She said she didn't want to stay with anybody; she just wanted to visit each of us. Didn't want to have to choose sides. She loved both of us. My conversation with her broke my heart. She didn't ask for any of this. I felt awful. Guilty, even. I said to her, "And we both love you. You know that don't you?"

"Yes."

"How 'bout this? You come and stay with me, and you can see your daddy whenever you like. I'll never try to keep you away from him. I promise."

"Kay."

With that the matter was settled. I had the kids; Hubbie had everything else. After my talk with my baby, I did get a legal separation. All I had to do was stay away from Hubbie sexually and the divorce petition could be filed at the end of one year.

I bought new furniture for my place. It was a small apartment, but it was comfortable enough for three. It was on the west side of town, about five miles from the house. On Saturday mornings the kids rode their bikes out to see their father. It worked fine for a while. Then they started coming home early because either Hubbie was not there or he was about to leave with his friend. So, the visits became less and less frequent until, finally, the girls stopped putting forth the effort to go.

Hubbie took to stopping by my apartment unannounced after that. I didn't lock the door when I slept during the day because the girls were always in and out. On one occasion I awoke to find him standing over me.

"What are you doing here?" I asked.

"Just came by to see the girls."

"Where are they?"

"Outside. Playing."

I didn't move. He wandered around the apartment for a minute and then came right back into my room. "Looks good in here. Who's helping you?"

"What?"

"Who's helping you buy this shit?"

"Nobody. I bought it myself."

"How come you're in here with the door unlocked?"

"Didn't see any reason to lock it until this moment."

He laughed at that. "Yeah. You oughta lock the door. Never can tell who might walk in here."

"You're right," I said. "I'll do that right now."

I got up and walked him to the door. Then I locked it behind him.

❁   ❁   ❁

On August 11, 1978, the girls wanted to go to the swimming pool. I still didn't have a car, and after calling three or four people who were all busy, I called Ronald and asked him to give them a ride. He came over immediately, and when he got ready to load them into his car, the baby girl remembered that she had left her bathing suit in the apartment. I had an uneasy feeling, and I begged her to hurry. She ran back to get her suit and while she was gone, Hubbie drove up to my door. He looked at me and he looked at Ronald. He said, "Thank you." He squinted his eyes and his top lip trembled. He repeated, "I wanna thank you, hear?"

I said, "Hubbie, don't. There is no trouble here. The kids just needed a ride to the pool.

"Thank you. I'll fix you."

He got into his car and took off, flying down the street like a madman. I knew he would come back. History had taught me that the threat was very real. I figured it was time for the showdown, and I didn't want my children to see it. I asked Ronald to take them on to the swimming pool. But I was

85

frightened, and I guess Ronald saw that. He convinced me to get into his car. We dropped off the kids and then we went to his apartment.

Half an hour later we saw Hubbie drive up. Ronald locked his door and took out his .357 magnum. I said, "Don't go to the door with the gun in your hand." So, he put it away and opened the door. Hubbie stormed in and grabbed me by the wrists, pulling me towards the door. He snatched me clean out of my shoes. Ronald said, "Look man, let's talk about this." Hubbie said, "I'm not going to hurt her. I just want to talk to her." Ronald said, " Now look man…" and picked up his gun. Hubbie said, "Guns don't scare me. She's my wife. I'm going to talk to her." I said, "Ronald, it's okay." Hubbie said, "Yeah. You tell him to back off."

It all happened so fast. Hubbie had me out the door in no time and into his car. He threw his leg across both of mine and popped me in the mouth. I screamed. He put the car in gear and drove off. He took me the long way to the house. Down Jackson Street. Turned right at Nash. All the way through uptown and downtown. Across the railroad tracks. Across Highway 301. Around Barnes Elementary School before he doubled back and went down Longview Drive. He beat me all the way. He was careful not to hit me in my face, but he pounded my arms, legs and stomach. He was talking pure shit the whole time:

"All this time I been waiting for you to come home! Here you are with him! I got news for you. If you want to be with that nigger you can. But you'll both be six feet under. 'Cause I'm going to kill yo' ass. But don't you worry none. I ain't gonna kill you here. I'm gonna take you home and kill you. Where you belong!"

Then I started talking shit:

"Fine. Kill me then. I'd rather be dead than stay with you!"

I started fighting back, too. For the first time in my life with him I got in a few good scratches, a couple of good slaps. That seemed to turn him on: "Aw, fighting back, huh bitch?" And he opened up a big can of whup ass then. We were fighting like dogs in the street while he drove. Car swerving all over everywhere. Folks on the sidewalk didn't know whether to shit or lay eggs. You should have seen them trying to get out of the way.

We reached the house and Hubbie went to unlock the door. "Don't you dare move," he said to me. Did he really think I was that crazy? I jumped out of the car and ran across the street. One of the neighbors was watering his lawn. I said, "Help me. Hubbie's going to kill me." The guy never put down his hose. Hubbie snatched me at the waist and picked me up. He carried me back across the street and threw me into the living room. He was wearing his Dingo boots, the ones with the steel toes. He kicked me from the front door into the kitchen. He picked me up and threw me down the stairs to the family room. Then he kicked me back upstairs. I scrambled to my feet and ran to a corner. I placed my hands on opposite walls and spread my feet wide. He could beat me all he wanted to, kill me even, but he was not going to knock me down again. He beat my clothes off of me. My earrings flew out of my ears. But I stayed on my feet and took it. That fueled his energy and his anger. "Where are your shoes?" he said. "You were getting ready to go to bed with him. I know it!"

Hubbie beat me that day until he was wet with sweat. When he finally stopped, he rushed upstairs. I thought he was going to get his gun. All of a sudden I wanted to live. It was then that I started to cry and beg for my life: "Please don't shoot me."

He had only gone to get a towel to wipe his face. But he said, "Naw. I ain't gonna shoot you. A trashy bitch like you don't deserve the time it would take to load the bullet."

I'm sure you've heard something like that before. In that movie about Tina Turner's life, *What's Love Got to Do With It?* Lorraine tells Tina something like that. But there is something about that line that attacks your self-esteem. It makes you want to defend yourself and your worth. Makes you want to say, "Yes I do. I deserve a bullet. Shoot me, goddammit!"

The telephone rang. It was our older daughter. "Let me speak to my mother," she said.

"What you gonna do if I don't? Beat me up?"

"I just want to speak with my mother."

Hubbie handed me the phone and my daughter asked if I was all right. I assured her that I was, but her call had stirred him up again. "Please don't call anymore," I said.

Next thing I know a police car pulled up in the driveway. Two cops rolled out leaving the door open. Hubbie opened the door of the house and stood between them and me. They could see me. They could see me good. But the three men stood outside by the police car and talked a little, laughed a little, and then the police left. I went into the kitchen and got the ice pick.

"One of your nosy neighbors told them that shots had been fired," he said. He then saw the ice pick. "Oh. Now you're going to kill yourself?"

I had no intentions of killing myself. My *self* had not done anything to me. But if he hit me one more time I was going to plant that pick deep into his chest.

"Come on," he said. "I'll take you home. I know you're not coming back to me now."

He took me to my apartment and left me on the sidewalk. I couldn't get into my place because my keys were in my purse, and my purse was at Ronald's. I went to a neighbor's house and called him. He told me that the kids were with him and they were safe. I should get a taxi over there.

Ronald took one look at me and started crying. He vowed to protect me from Hubbie. We both suffered that night. I'd panic every time I heard a car pull into the driveway. Aside from that, I was injured. I kept getting flashes of light in my right eye. My left arm was swollen to three times its normal size. My legs were in bad shape from the kicks. I could not walk. Ronald had to lift me and set me on the toilet whenever I had to pee. I was bruised everywhere. Footprints were all over my back and legs. When I went to the doctor the next day, my backbone was dislocated in seven places.

But something good always comes out of something bad. When my parents heard about it, they came to Ronald's apartment to see me. My father was fit to be tied. He and Mama told me to stay where I was for a couple of days. When I got better, my daddy took me to the police station and he filed a complaint against the officers who left me at Hubbie's house. That's when I found out the way the law worked in domestic violence cases. "All you had to do," the Chief said, "Was walk past him to get to get to one of our men. If he had done anything then, we would have been able to arrest him. Without that, it's your word against his because we didn't see anything happen."

From there I went to see my lawyer and tried to get a restraining order. She told me that the law didn't work that way. There was really nothing anyone could do until after he killed me. But she did offer some sound advice: "You had every right to be where you were. A legal separation is not one-sided. If he has freedom of movement, so do you."

"I wasn't doing anything that time."

"It doesn't matter. But the way he has beaten and threatened you, you could blow him away, and you'd never spend a day in jail."

I didn't want to hurt Hubbie any more than I wanted him to continue hurting me. After that last beating, though, I took to carrying a .357 magnum in my purse, and I kept my shotgun next to my bed. If he approached me on the job and I saw the need to defend myself, I wasn't going to fuck around with it. I would *kill* him. I *would* kill him. I would.

A guy I knew from high school was a supervisor at work. He came to my machine one day and tried to "talk" to me about what I was doing. He said Hubbie really loved me. Said I was being selfish. He said he just didn't know what was wrong with women nowadays. They get the nice houses and fancy cars, then they want to leave their husbands. I told him that it was none of his business and he should stay out of it. He went right back and told Hubbie. Next thing I know, here he comes talking trash:

"You've changed! You used to listen to folks that's got good damn sense. You need to bring yo' ass home!"

I looked at that man that day and I saw a whining, complaining, evil little boy who could not accept any responsibility for the things he did. I determined that he was afraid of himself, so he had to cover up his fear by taking it out on me. I thought about Jessie: "She tricked me," he'd said. "I just went over there to fix her TV." I thought about how he tried to keep me prisoner in his little kingdom. I thought about his addiction to sex. I thought about the times I gave him babies, and the doctor said no sex for six weeks. How he begged, "Just let me put the head in." And how mad he got when I refused. Oh yes, I thought about all that, and there was nothing—no thing that could make me go back to that.

He tried to bully me into going back to him every day. In the same breath he'd let me know how happy he was with his girlfriend. He'd come to my machine at work, jump into my car at the traffic light, speed past me on the road home so I could see him turning onto his lady's street. I felt somewhat protected at work, but I never knew when he would catch me alone and try something. I was scared and nervous all the time when I was at home. I was dropping weight at the rate of two pounds a day. I could hardly function. So I sold my furniture and moved in with Ronald, for protection.

The very next day I was warned by a co-worker that Hubbie was on his way to my machine. I tried to run, but he was right there. Fuming. Huffing and puffing about what all he was going to do:

"What the fuck is wrong with you? You crazy or something? I woulda never thought you'd do some stupid shit like this. I don't want my kids around that mother fucker! You-get-my-kids-out-of-that-house-by-four-o'clock-today! Or, I got news for you and him! Matter of fact, I'm going over there to tell him right now!"

He stormed away from me then and charged towards Ronald's station. I freaked. Hubbie and I had lived together for almost a year before we married. In the fifteen years we'd been together, he had screwed everything that wasn't nailed down. Now that I was gone, he didn't have time for his children because he was busy chasing a cat. Now all of a sudden he was trying to be downright righteous? That was inconceivable to me.

I summoned the foreman and I noticed that he came quickly. "Call the cops," I said. Hubbie's going over to get Ronald."

"He already got him. Come on. Let's go."

The foreman took me to a conference room and sat with me for a very long time. After about an hour he left me there locked up in that room for a few minutes. When he came back he told me what had happened. Hubbie walked up to Ronald and hit him. Ronald hit back and the fight was on. They tussled for a while with everyone standing around watching. Then Ronald slipped and fell against the rack that holds the tires. His head split open. Somebody grabbed Hubbie from behind, and they ushered him out of the building. Security took Ronald to ER where they stitched his wound. The managers fired both of them on the spot.

The foreman escorted me out of the room and delivered me directly to Ronald. His head was bloody and bandaged. The bosses decided not to give us a police escort home because this had started outside the plant and they couldn't jeopardize the life of their employees.

The awful nightmare of a man chasing me with a gun interrupted my sleep almost every night by now. I still didn't know what to make of it until that day. As we pulled into Ronald's parking lot, it suddenly dawned on me that it was the exact location of my dream. I stayed awake all night. The next day, my dream came true.

✾ ✾ ✾

Ronald and I were sitting in the living room trying to decide what to do next. I wanted to move far away. He wanted to file an appeal and get his job back. "We can stay here," he said. "Hubbie will get the message after a while. It'll be tough, but we can make it. We can have a good life together."

We heard a car drive up. It was Hubbie. Ronald told me to go out the back door and get to a neighbor's apartment across the court. For the first time in my life I did exactly as I was told. I ran out the back door and along the side of the building. The complex was two parallel lines with a curve of grass at one end. When I got to the parking lot, I stopped and looked at Ronald's front door. My heart was beating so fast I thought I would throw it up. Hubbie was standing on Ronald's front porch, but he was looking toward the street, so his back was to me. I ran across the parking lot and down the back of the other side. I saw the three garbage cans, but I knew they were there because of the dream. I did not stumble over them. Rather, I lay down on the patio of the apartment next to them and started banging on the door. I could hear the phone ringing inside, but the woman opened her back door first. Her name was Ruby. She saved my life.

The caller on the phone was Ronald, and he told her that Hubbie was at his door. He begged her to hide me, and she did. Even when Hubbie knocked on her door, she didn't answer it. After a while he went away.

He never bothered me again after that. Not really. He threatened to kill Mama and Daddy because they let me wash clothes at their house. He threatened to kill Ruby because she gave me a ride to work. He called a couple of times. One time he cried like a wounded animal. Didn't want to talk; just wanted me to hear him cry. When I hung up the phone he was still crying. Another time, after I'd bought my own car, he jumped in when I stopped at the traffic light. He sat in that house for six months and refused to pay a dime on the mortgage. He put an article in the newspaper that said, "I refuse to be responsible for any debts other than those incurred by myself." He even wrote a letter to Dear Abby: "Is it possible to forgive and forget?—Hubbie." But he never tried to physically hurt me again.

We were divorced in September of 1979. The only thing he contested was child support. I didn't want anything from him. I certainly didn't want alimony. But the judge said that I could not waive child support, and that held up the proceedings. Hubbie's pay on his new job was just over six hundred dollars a month. I told my lawyer that he could not afford to help me raise these children in the manner to which they have become accustomed, imitating the way the judge had said it. But my lawyer said, "Fuck 'im. And feed 'im beans." So the judge granted the divorce and awarded me forty dollars a week in child support.

Hubbie and I shook hands after court, as if we were honoring some competitive sports event. I think I said something stupid like, "Nice knowing you." But he said, "Congratulations. You're free to do whatever you want now. I hope you enjoy your life."

"Well, I will certainly try to," I told him, and at long last, we went our separate ways.

sixteen

Forty dollars is not a lot of money, but it can have a great impact on one's life when it is received as child support. The girls thought I should divide it between them. I thought it should go towards their little incidentals--skating rink, movies, basketball uniforms. Ronald had been reinstated on his job, so financially, my life had not changed very much at all. With no mortgage and little else to worry about, we had plenty of money. Plenty of money. We had money in the bank, in coffee cans, in the top dresser drawer. A shoe box full of bonds. But I wanted to teach the girls some responsibility about money. I wanted them to know that they had to earn their way through life, so I gave them chores and used the forty dollars to pay them for the work they did. Ronald agreed with them, and it became one of the little issues that caused long and sometimes heated discussions. He said he didn't want anything in his house that belonged to Hubbie. I laughed at that, considering the circumstance that Hubbie's entire family lived there. My laughter made Ronald angry, but he pretty much conceded and let me raise my children the way I saw fit.

We loved…hard. Couldn't keep our hands off each other. As soon as the kids left for school, we went at it. I'd take a shower and before I'd get from the bathroom to the bedroom, he'd have me pinned against the wall, or on the toilet seat or the floor. I loved the spontaneity, and I loved him. I didn't need a big fancy house; loving him was enough for me. He gave me the good things in life. Made me aware of the smell of the air, the different colors of birds in the yard. It reminded me of when I was a child walking barefoot on ground that had been freshly sprinkled with the first spring rain—the feel of it, the fragrance, made me want to eat the dirt. It was a new beginning. I knew I could count on him. And for one brief, precious moment in history, I was happy. Weak. Very weak. But very, very happy.

But all that good loving began to interfere with my work. After a while I just couldn't keep up. I had gained my weight back, but I was tired all the time. My period had been acting funny. I was on the pill, had a twenty-one day cycle, and my period was due at three o'clock in the afternoon of the scheduled day. It showed up right on time, but it was just…different. Sometimes it lasted a week; sometimes it lasted two days. I went to a doctor and, after a few tests, he gave me the news: I was pregnant. Four whole months! My baby girl was thirteen years old and there I was starting all over again. I behaved so poorly when I got that news, they kept me overnight for *observation.*

Of course, Ronald was beside himself with joy. "I made that my goal!" he said to me. I could only imagine what it did for his man thing. Getting me pregnant while I was on the pill empowered him. And he was good to me; I have to admit that. There was no limit to what he would do for me. I had to go on disability because the job was too hard on my body. But Ronald would work all day and then come home and cook. He wouldn't let me do a thing; he really wanted that baby. After the amniocentesis and we learned that it was a boy, well, I sat on satin pillows all day with my feet propped up.

But my history with Hubbie had made me acutely aware of small offenses. I didn't want to compare the two men, but I couldn't help noticing little things that Ronald did. There seemed to be a kind of universal sense of entitlement in the male-female relationship and he had all the privileges, all the power. Standing alone these *little things* didn't mean a whole lot, but together they began to grate on my nerves. He'd take my car and leave his sitting in the driveway. I couldn't drive his car, so I was stuck at home until he returned. He tried to tell me how to raise my kids. I didn't feel isolated in my protest because I don't know *any* black women who will allow that. He opened my mail before I could get to it, sometimes right in front of me, and he'd decide what was important enough for me to read. He didn't want me to wear makeup; he liked me "plain." He didn't want me to wear dresses because "Ain't nobody 'spose to see your legs but me." I could not wear high heels because, "Baby, when two people walk down the street, one ain't 'spose to be taller than the other one. They 'spose to be the same height." But he wore high heels, though, to give himself the illusion that he was as tall as I. He had a fit because my children wouldn't call him "Daddy." He said he didn't like steak, so one day when I cooked steak for the kids and me, I made pork chops for him. He accused me of making him feel like he was not a part of the family. He's a damned Gemini. Two entirely different people. It got to the point where I didn't know which one was coming at me, so I stayed on guard.

The baby grew to be huge and, naturally, the love sessions slowed down a bit. That's when I discovered that Ronald and I didn't agree on anything. I didn't want a house, but we got a house. All new furniture that he picked out. I didn't want to get married. We argued about that. He did the laundry because I didn't do it properly. I took the girls school shopping one day and stayed three hours. When I got back he had called the law. Said he was afraid something had happened to us. And God forbid if I was on the phone when he came home from work: "Who you in there yakkin' to? Get off."

Of course, I stayed dead on his ass about every little thing. I wasn't about to go through another Hubbie. But whenever I tried to talk with Ronald, he'd cry. Then I'd scold him about that, and he'd cry more. And he was so melodramatic. Once, after an argument, he ran out of the house and got in my car. As he was driving away, in *my* car, he said, "Baby, if you don't ever see me again, just remember, I love you." The shit was so funny, I couldn't even be angry anymore, so I told him to come on back in the house.

The problem, as I saw it, was that Hubbie had used up all my patience for a man. Shame. Ronald didn't have a chance. Just like Yeats said, things fall apart…

I began to question myself, my place in the universe. I didn't know myself very well. I located and identified what I wanted based on what I didn't want. I decided that the only way I could become complete was to go back to school. I would go over to Atlantic Christian College and take some classes. I wanted to study philosophy and art. History and music. Anthropology. Geography. Not necessarily to accumulate a bunch of degrees, but to become *educated*. I told Ronald about my plans and, you know, it never dawned on me that I needed his permission. He said he would allow me to do that as long as I was willing to wait until the baby arrived.

My water broke at 6:30 on a Sunday night. My son was not born until 11:29 Wednesday morning. During that time I discovered why it is called "labor." My doctor had assured me that I would get something to help me with the pain. I'd had a spinal tap with both my girls before I went into active labor. I was young then. Now, I was thirty-five years old, and I was frightened. That button-head boy took his time coming through the cave, and by the time my doctor arrived at 11:27, the pain had me in its grip. I couldn't breathe. Couldn't do anything but scream. They had me strapped to the delivery bed. The nurse threatened to slap me for making so much noise, but she backed off when I asked her if she liked her hand. My doctor had not told them to give me anything, and when he strolled in I begged him to help me. He said, "It's all on you now, kid. You brought this on yourself." Can you imagine a doctor saying something like that to a patient? Neither can I, but it's the truth. That's exactly what he said, as if he wanted to punish me and all women for some reason.

My son weighed in at almost nine pounds. One thing I learned from this whole experience, though I didn't know at the time that I would need this knowledge, is that once the baby pops out, the pain stops. I learned something else, too. It's called "labor" because you have to work. You have to force that child out of you because babies have more sense than we do. They don't want to leave their own little private, secure world and come into one that alienates them from the start.

When we brought the baby home from the hospital, Ronald behaved like Mufasa, presenting his young prince to society. He walked the child through the house and introduced him to every room. He'd sit for hours admiring that boy, talking to him. Talking *for* him: "I look just like my daddy. I look just like my daddy. Don't I Ma?" He bathed and dressed him twice a day. All I had to do was feed him. When the baby cried in the middle of the night, Ronald was the first to hit the floor. He took vacation time from work so he could be home with us. And when he went back to work, he'd rush home to hold his son.

But it all came crashing down when I was scheduled to return to work a month later. During the time I had been on leave, Ronald had handled all the bills. Our bank account had dwindled to practically nothing, so I had to go back to work. I was also planning to keep my promise about college, and I expected Ronald to keep his.

Two days before I went back to work, I told Ronald that I would be late coming home because I wanted to stop by the college and get a catalog. He got up early the next morning and left the house in my car. When he came back he said that he had enrolled in Wilson Tech. Said he should get his education first, and he asked me if I was proud of him. I didn't say anything because I was in shock, I guess. Anyway, he had to go back that afternoon to choose his classes, and he did, except that when he returned he was walking.

"Somebody stole the car, Babe," he said.

I don't remember a whole lot of that conversation. But I do remember asking him if he had called the police.

"No. I hadn't even thought about that. I just came straight home."

It seemed to me that the police would be first to know if somebody stole your shit. *My shit.* So I reached for the phone and he stood there with his eyes in the top of his head, thinking.

"Wait a minute," he said. "Maybe it wasn't stolen. I can't remember the last time I made a payment on it. You think the bank would repossess it?"

I can't tell you how I felt about him at that moment. I have yet to be able to identify it. I recognized even then that there is something about me that strips a man of his backbone. It was not about the car; surely I could get another one. It wasn't even about money. From the time I was seven years old I have been able to generate enough money to satisfy my needs. I did not believe that money could make me happy, even though I was convinced that the lack of it could be a major source of misery. It was about the untimely inconvenience and interference in my life. I hope you truly understand what I mean when I say that. It was not the baby, but the pregnancy that was inconvenient. I loved to work. I was raised to work. Hell, I'd have about fifty babies if we could figure out a way to microwave them or something, get them done in a shorter time so I would not have to stop working. Maybe I am selfish, I thought. But it seemed to me that if I could go through with having our son, if I could put up with the whole town gossiping about me, if I could put my whole life on hold just to satisfy his ego, the very least he could do was pay the freaking car note!

I had been raised to believe that woman as an un-manned vessel is worthless. In my search for reasons to stay with Ronald I found myself doing hardcore comparisons between him and Hubbie: Hubbie would bring his paycheck home and take an "allowance" of fifty dollars every payday. Ronald liked to have his money in his pocket, so that at a poker game when the stakes were high, he could imitate Richard Pryor: "Is that a hunderd dollar bill? Is that a hunerd dollar bill?" And the poor guy who delivers his check to his wife twice a month would shrink back and say, "Yeah, that's a hunerd."

In fifteen years of marriage Hubbie only cooked for me once, a week before I left him: steak, baked potato and a salad. Ronald cooked four or five times a week: fried chicken, French fries and rice; fried pork chops, French fries and rice; barbequed chicken French fries and rice. He didn't like anything green. He bitched every time I came home from the grocery story. And I was spending *my* money. Hubbie never bought personal gifts. Ronald bought so many flowers I got sick of them. Hubbie did not dance, drink, smoke or play cards. Ronald did all of the above in excess. I had thought he was what I wanted—a man who was alive and knew how to enjoy his life. Hubbie was a slow leak.

But I began to see that Ronald was not what I wanted, either. He was as rigid in his flexibility as Hubbie was flexible in his rigidity. I understood that I had left one man and got with another before I had a chance to discover myself. It was a simple trade-in for a newer model. I had thought that going to college would provide some answers for me, but now, with the car gone, that college dream had to be deferred again.

It slowly dawned on me that we had nothing in common except our son. I thought we were a team, equal partners on the same side. But I was soon to learn that one of us was just a little bit more equal than the other. Ronald became extremely possessive once he got me. If a man came to visit and didn't bring his lady, I had to leave the room. If I was wearing shorts when company came, I had to change my clothes. We had a four-day weekend every month, but I was never allowed to choose how we would spend it. I liked the beach; Ronald, a former sailor, hated the ocean. One day I put my foot down and told Ronald that I wanted to go to Myrtle Beach for the weekend.

"I don't want to go there, Babe."

"Why not?"

"Because that's where you always went with Hubbie. I don't want to do anything like him."

"Well…where do you want to go?"

"Carowinds."

"Are we taking the kids?"

"No. Let's just you and me go. Have a little fun. We both could use a break. The kids will be all right."

We did need a break, so I decided to compromise.

"Okay. Carowinds it is. But I want you to promise me one thing.

"Anything. You name it."

"Either on our way there, or on our way back, I want to have dinner at Red Lobster."

"Deal."

I planned and organized things for two whole weeks. What I didn't know at the time was that Ronald had invited another couple to join us. The woman of that couple and I did not like each other at all; we just put up a front because our men were such good friends. But this was supposed to be our weekend. So, when Ronald turned the car to the north towards Rocky Mount, I complained.

"Take me back home! I don't want to be around her at work, I know I don't want to spend a whole weekend with her!"

"You don't have to spend any more time with her than you choose to, but we are not going back home. Everything is all arranged."

We argued all the way to Rocky Mount. I was hot. And it looked like the madder I got the calmer he became, until finally, I realized that I was fussing by myself.

"Well, I tell you one damned thing," I told him. "I just better get that lobster."

It was early morning when we set out for Charlotte, and once we got there, the excitement of the park took hold. We stayed for two nights, and I actually had a good time in spite of myself and the rest of our company. We came back on Sunday, and we decided not to eat breakfast, but rather, stop and get something on the road when we got hungry. Ronald drove and drove. About three o'clock in the afternoon, as we were passing through Raleigh, everybody started to complain about their stomachs growling. Ronald said, "What y'all wanna eat?" And I said, "Oh, there's no question. We're going to Red Lobster." I had a big smile on my face. But Ronald said, "It's too early to go to Red Lobster, Babe. Let's go grab a burger." And *she* said, "Yeah. Don't nobody want no damn lobster."

Just like that, the matter was settled. Ronald pulled into Hardee's, which is right across the street from Red Lobster. I felt totally defeated, but my pride made me go in and try to eat that dry cheeseburger. I was not successful in that attempt. Ronald teased me: "Lookathere…don't that hamburger taste just like lobster? Lookathere." The three of them laughed so heartily, it made me lose my appetite. At that moment I hated him. He had humiliated me in front of her. It was her husband who saw my hurt: "Ron, you 'sposed to take care of yo' baby, man."

Trifling. Ronald was just plain trifling.

You know…in her book, *Their Eyes Were Watching God,* Zora Neale Hurston uses Janie Crawford to deliver a heavy message. Now, there's a woman who looks for happiness through a man all her life, and then suddenly she realizes the real source of happiness. She tells her friend, Phoebe, "Two things everybody's got tuh do fuh theyselves. They got tuh go tuh God, and they got tuh find out about livin' fuh theyselves." I knew I had to go to God because it looked like God was not going to come to me. I think I knew at that moment that I was going to escape. I could not find out about *me* as long as I stayed in Wilson. And just like Janie says, "You got tuh go there tuh *know* there," nobody could do anything for me. I had to figure it out myself. I had to re-write the script and find meaning and purpose in God's blueprint for my life.

The first step was to try to reconnect with God. Oh, I knew He was pissed; He had every right to be. But the Bible teaches that if you come back to Him, He'll take you in. I decided to go Mama's church to see if I could find salvation.

seventeen

I will admit I went with a heavy heart. It wasn't like the first time I joined church. The first time I was only ten years old and all I wanted to do then was sing in the junior choir. The only way to get into the choir was to be a member of the church and Reverend Jordan was very strict about that rule.

I often reminisce about that day. I told Mama that I was going to join church and she said, "Have you had ...*the feeling?*" I didn't want to lie to her, so I just didn't answer, but I had no idea what she meant. Old people like Sister Henrietta must have had the feeling because they would stomp and shout. Sometimes folks would cut up so...raising their hands in the air and passing out, and all that was really funny to me, so I'd put my hand over my mouth to keep from laughing out loud in church. But now, I was determined to sing in that choir, so when the senior choir sang "Come Ye Disconsolate," and Reverend Jordan asked, "Is there one?" I marched down front and took a seat.

Three weeks later, my mother took me by the hand and led me into the church for my baptism. There were a dozen of us waiting to have our souls cleansed. Since I was the last to join church, I was the last to be baptized. I wore a waltz-length, white cotton dress and a white scarf over my head. My mother sat close to me in the row behind the baptismal candidates. One by one I watched the others being dipped into the water. Mama leaned forward and said, "Try not to choke. They say your soul ain't right with God if you choke." If God hadn't forgiven me for whatever dark spot there may have been on my soul, I sure hoped He wouldn't pick my baptism to show it. It would be such an embarrassment to my mother.

We'd left the house in a hurry that morning and I didn't have time to pee or eat breakfast before we set out to walk the two miles to the church. Roundtree Missionary Baptist Church was located on the east side of town, across Highway 301. It still had an old baptismal pool in the front yard even though we now had an indoor pool. At that time there was an outhouse that separated the church from the back end of Rest Haven Cemetery.

99

It was a dry, hot, early summer day. The mothers of the church cooled themselves with the cardboard fans from Hamilton Funeral Home. I was nervous. My stomach felt weak and empty. My mouth was dry, my bladder full, and that constant splashing of water…

I asked my mother if I could go to the toilet.

"Well, run on," she said. "But make haste."

I ran outside and headed for the outhouse, pushing down my underwear on the way. The heat shimmered across the graveyard and made it look like the spirits were dancing. Speed was of utmost importance, just in case the dead people decided to walk across the patch of grass that separated the churchyard from the graveyard. I flung the door open and sat down quickly. The relief was so good it made my eyes cross. I reached for the toilet paper and there was none. That's when I noticed the ants. A trail of red ants traveled from the tree next to the toilet, to the floor, the seat, and on up the wall. I fixed my clothes and ran back inside, the pee already saturating my bloomers.

By the time I reached my place nearly everyone in the church had gotten *the feeling*. Feet stomped. Hands waved in the air. Old ladies passed out. The church seemed to rock with a rhythm of its own. Sister Henrietta, watching her nephew being plunged into the water, kicked off her shoes and went into a frenzy of a shout—a cross between the Jitter Bug and an Indian war dance. Heat rose in that little church. Moisture clung to the walls, the windows and the pews. Drops of sweat ran from my armpits and tickled my sides. I felt a stinging sensation on my wet bottom. It moved upwards and out, covering my back and neck. I shivered. And then, remembering the ants, I began to fidget.

"Be still!" Mama said. "You'll be up pretty soon." She broke a stick of Juicy Fruit in half and put a piece into her mouth. I listened for my name. Mama twisted her handkerchief around her index finger and dabbed at her tongue. I tried to move away, but she held me by the shoulder. She cleaned my eyes and ears with her Juicy Fruit flavored spit.

I started to scratch.

"Stop that!" Mama whispered through clenched teeth. "Yes Jesus!" *"You're behaving like a two-year old!"* "Have mercy Lord." *"Don't make me get a hold of you right here in this church!"* "Praise God."

But I couldn't stop. The ants nibbled at my butt and thighs. I felt like my whole body was going through electric shock. Tears swelled in my eyes and spilled over, carrying the perfume of Juicy Fruit all over my face.

The preacher sang, " Take me to the wah-hor-hor-tuh…"

I stood up, scratching and squeezing my knees together. My hands shot forward, upward, and I hopped on one foot. I arched my back and folded myself into my own arms, scratching and pulling at my dress.

Voices in the congregation grew louder. All eyes were on me.

"Miracle child!"

"It's the Holy Ghost!"

"Hallelujah!"

And the preacher sang, "Take me to the wah-hor-hor-tuh…"

I stood there dancing—my fingers digging at the skin on my back, my legs, my arms. I lifted the hem of my dress, took off my shoes, and moved into the aisle.

"Take me to the wah-hor-hor-hor-hor-tuh…"

I jumped up and down, up and down, wriggling my hips, trying to shake the ants free of my wet bloomers. Sister Henrietta locked her arm into mine. Together we did a dosey-do in the aisle. There was a thunderous stomping of feet as the congregation expressed their joy.

"Barbara Ann Williams?"

"To be baptized."

I ran to the front of the church and eagerly stepped into the baptismal pool. The congregation leaped to their feet.

"Praise the Lord!"

Reverend Jordan placed one hand on my back, the other on my stomach. "In the name of the Father…" I bent my knees, my body still twitching. "and of the Son…" I took a deep breath and closed my eyes. *Please God let him hurry up!* "…and of the Holy Ghost…" He dipped me into the water. "A-men!"

The water, cool and soothing to my body, enveloped me. I believed I could hold my breath forever if only I could keep that feeling. Reverend Jordan tried to lift me. I stiffened and refused to let him take me out of the water. I felt him nudge me, gently, but I held onto him. He put his arm under my knees and in one quick motion, he snatched me out of the water. I emerged feeling satisfied, exhausted.

"Amen!" I said. "Thank you Jee-sus! A-hay-yay-men!"

A line of people waited for me. They all touched me, passing me from one to the other until I reached my mother in the choir room. She wrapped a towel around me and sat down, pulling me to her lap. She tucked my head under her neck and cradled me in her arms. We held each other for a long, long time.

But it wasn't like that this time. It wasn't about the people in the church. I went to the church and sat in the back. I had left that church partly because I had moved away from Wilson, but mostly because I thought there were devils there. Brothers and sisters would go to pray all day long on Sundays, but the rest of the week they were just as mean and sneaky as snakes. They try to tell others how to live their lives in a Christian way, but they won't share a meal if one is hungry; they won't give a dime if one is broke. They go home right after church and talk about what this one wore and what that one said. And all the while they are grinning in someone's face: "How you Sister So and So?" They hope to hear of some crisis that they have no interest in helping solve.

No. *It* wasn't about them. My son was a sickly child, and I was awake practically all night every night taking care of him. It got me to the point where I had to force myself to go to work. I'd sit on the edge of my bed and cry because I had to go to work. The only thing that kept me going was the knowledge that so many folks were unemployed. It was a bad time. People were going to jail for stealing food. A girl on Church Street stabbed her brother in the heart with a fork, killed him dead, because he tried to take her pork chop. 1981 was a hard year for everyone I knew. Still, going to work was a chore. Then, one night, I dreamed that the place caught fire and out of two thousand employees, I was the only one who couldn't get out.

It wasn't about *them*. I left Ronald and moved into an apartment. Giving him up was the hardest thing I had ever had to do because I truly loved him. But I came to see him for what he really was, and love was not enough. Ronald was a tool, an instrument that gave me the courage I needed to get away from Hubbie. That's all. We didn't have the glue to keep our love together. If it were not him, it would have been somebody else. The point was that I had to get away from Hubbie by any means necessary. Ronald served that purpose.

It was not *about* them. I was weak with exhaustion and I stayed sick all the time. I quit my job, but I found out that without a job I couldn't even borrow five dollars to buy Pampers for my baby. It was true what my girl-friends said to me as they sent me to their husbands when I needed a favor: *Well, Barbara, you know you brought this on yourself.* Yes. I had made my bed, as they say, and now I had to wallow in it.

It was *not* about them. After I left Ronald I discovered that I was pregnant again. He advised me to get an abortion *(Since we ain't together or nothing),* and I let him talk me into that. At that time I had not given any thought to the moral issues about abortion. But I lay on that table and felt all the guilt and burdens of the whole world. I was afraid to sleep. Afraid God would kill me. I was afraid to stay awake. Afraid that I would die anyway and be conscious of it. The memory of that slurping sound, like a wet vacuum cleaner, haunts me to this day. It is the only thing I have ever done in my whole life that I regret, and I believe I'll have to account for it when St. Peter calls me.

Itwasnotaboutthem. My oldest child was pregnant, too. Everybody wanted to get in that: *Watcha gone do? Ain't it a shame? Mama and daughter both? I hear you trying to make huh git rid of it!* But nobody offered any real advice, and they damn sure didn't offer any money. When I called my Mama's house to speak to my father, she said he was busy peeling potatoes. He did not come to the phone.

It…was…not…about…them. It was about *me* and my beliefs.

I believe in God. I believe He is a man. But I also believe He has woman qualities. God is a nurturer *and* a protector. God never said that Eve was evil; man said that. And man never took the responsibility for his own shortcomings. "She tricked me," Adam said. Well, whatever he said, that's what he meant.

I believe that God gave man brute strength because of the work he was supposed to do. And I think it pisses God off every time man turns that strength against his woman.

I believe that God wants some people to suffer, the better to make them whole. I believe I am one of those chosen few, and suffering has made me the composite woman I am today.

I believe that God, alone, decides when enough is enough, and He sends a sign to let us know when it is time for a change. He already sent one of His children here to absorb the sins of the world. He's got other plans for me. That dream about the fire? That was my sign.

It *was* not about them.

It was about freedom. I had to escape the prison of the mind. My mother and her mother and her mother and hers were all in prison because some man rewrote the rules of God's intent. I'm telling you, girls…we've been spoon fed the poison of inferiority, and too many of us swallow it whole. That stuff in the Bible about a woman's place was written by men, so naturally it suits their purposes. Yet, even if we do subscribe to it through some martyr-oriented sense of sacrifice, how do we reconcile the notion that the dominant male is willing to let his wife work and support him, or be a slave

103

to him, when the Bible clearly says that they are equal parts of one whole? Let me give an example: As long as I remember it has been preached to me to "Remember the Sabbath and keep it Holy." My mother would not let me shine my shoes or plant flowers or cut my hair on Sunday because the Bible says you're not supposed to work on Holy day. But we could cook at home and at church. We could sew a button on a shirt for our husband or brother. We could even clean up the house and the church on Sunday. If I've heard it once, I've heard it a thousand times: *How dare you sit there with a book in your hand when you know there are beds to be made, floors to be swept, dishes to be washed?* All on Sunday. Now. I ask you…ain't that work? Hell, we could even take a beating on Sunday.

It was about time. A famous poet once wrote: "When you take my time, you're taking something I had planned to use." The way I saw it, I had served my sentence. Fifteen years of hard labor with Hubbie. Three years of probation with Ronald. All that for a crime I did not commit. Now I needed rehab. You can't expect a drug addict to be cured by placing her in a pharmacy. Overeaters will never be able to resist the urge if they work in a restaurant. How's an alcoholic going to get cured if he drinks *café royale?* We all have to make changes before it is too late. I was wasting my time in Wilson. I believed that I could do something important. When you think about it, only the very good or the very bad go down in the history books. If you are not a Martin, Malcolm or Ghandi; Harriet, Sojourner or Jean D'Arc; if you're not a Jesse James, Al Capone or Napolean, historians don't give a shit about you. Nobody knows your name. I did not want to live my life anonymously. I didn't want to spend the rest of my life thinking about woulda shoulda coulda. I wanted my life to mean something, and give my children a foundation from which they could build.

It was about *love.* God helps those who help themselves. I've read a lot of stuff about Black women and self-hatred. Folks who write that nonsense don't know us. They have never lived our lives or survived the horrors of triple discrimination. Though He gave me a cross to bear, God didn't mean for me to be crucified just because I am woman. And whether you believe in Jesus, Moses, Mohammed or a head of lettuce, God is an equal opportunity protector.

It was about my children. They had every right to expect a sane and healthy mother to help them with their problems. I didn't want them to be crippled by the kind of life I led.

Finally, it was about survival. I knew that if I stayed there, I would die there, without ever having lived at all. I survived all I had been through with

Hubbie, and that was proof that God wanted me to live.

I began to see fear as a wasted emotion. Such a waste. The fear of God is the only one that counts. I made plans to leave the state. My cousin, Shug, lived in Vacaville, California. When I called him and told him about my situation he said, "Sure…come on. We'll take care of you Barbr'ann."

In *Song of Solomon* Morrison lets Guitar say something profound: "Wanna fly? You got to get rid of the shit that weighs you down." I sold or gave away everything I owned except our clothes. I even sold a Curtis Mathis television set for two hundred dollars. Of course, Ronald had a fit about that because we had paid twelve hundred for it. But I didn't want anything to weigh me down. I just wanted to get the hell out of there, as far away as I could get and start my life anew.

I collected just enough money to get me where I wanted to go. Once I had four bus tickets in my hand, I packed my things and moved to California. At the time I didn't know whether I was running *to* or running *from* or just plain running. Period. But my hatred for the known completely overwhelmed the questions of the unknown. And for the first time in almost twenty years, I was not afraid.

PART II
ESCAPE

eighteen

It was a good thing to leave at night. My son was too young to know what was happening, but the girls cried themselves to sleep. When they awoke, we were in a part of the country they had never seen: Western Maryland, with its beautiful, rolling green hills. By the time we reached West Virginia, they were singing "California, here I come!"

I had cried, too. Never was any good at saying goodbyes. Deep down in my heart I knew that Mama and Daddy loved me, but I could not live my life for them anymore. They knew that. They *knew* that, and getting away from Wilson…well, it was a good thing.

My sister took it harder than anyone. I was practically her mother. I was fourteen years and one week old when she was born, and since Mama worked, I was the one who took care of her for the first four years of her life. She was such a puny little thing. She only weighed two pounds when she was born, and then she lost about six ounces. It took her two months to reach five pounds so we could bring her home.

I enjoyed taking care of her. I used to bathe her, dress her up in bows and frills, and put her on the front porch so she could get some sun. She was the color of a half-baked biscuit; you could see her little veins through her skin. Hard as I tried, I could not make her gain weight. When she was ten months old, she only weighed ten pounds, and she was constantly sick.

We almost lost her two or three times before she was a year old. She didn't do things that other babies did. I mean, she just didn't try to do anything. Never reached for a piece of food, never said *da-da*, never even tried to sit up.

We thought it was because she was a premie. But there were other babies in our neighborhood who were born after she was and they were doing all kinds of things. Some of them were walking already. Felise kept getting weaker and weaker until finally, Mama took her to see Dr. Ryburn. At that time he donated one day a week at Mercy Hospital, the one for colored people. Dr. Ryburn told Mama that the baby had pneumonia and was severely anemic. "She has practically no blood. She'll need a transfusion right away," he said.

Mama started wringing her hands. "Just give me the papers ," she said. "I'll sign them. I'll pay for it."

"No. No, you don't understand. It's not quite that simple. She has a very rare blood type--AB negative. We don't have that kind of blood here."

"Well, where can I get it?"

"I don't know. But if you don't find some, I'm afraid this baby won't make it through the night."

That took all the starch out of Mama. She had already lost Cornell to pneumonia. She sat right down in the middle of the floor and cried.

Mr. Charles James, who owned and operated Darden Funeral Home, saw Mama wailing, and he asked if he could help. She told him about Felise and he put Mama in his car and drove her around town, knocking on doors, looking for AB negative blood. They searched for about four hours, and finally, they went to the poolroom downtown--a place Mama would never go under normal circumstances. There was a man there whose name was Johnny Oates. He said he had O positive blood, which made him a universal donor.

"I don't have a dime to pay you," Mama said. "But if you will give my baby a pint, just a pint, I will be so grateful."

"Yes Ma'am," he said. "Take all you need."

Mr. Oates got in the car with Mama and Mr. James and they went to the hospital. He had to drink some coffee because he had been drinking alcohol. He gave two pints of blood, drank some orange juice and left, never to be seen or heard from again.

The medical staff started the transfusion immediately and Dr. Ryburn told Mama to go home and get some rest. That was about six o'clock that evening. At eleven o'clock, Uncle Shird came to the house and said that Dr. Ryburn wanted to see Mama . She jumped out of bed and took off running. When she came back two hours later, her oldest sister, Aunt Aileen was with her. It looked like Aunt Aileen was holding Mama to keep her from falling. I was afraid to ask the question, but I knew I had to know. "Mama, is Felise dead?"

"Naw…not yet."

Then Aunt Aileen said something I never forgot or forgave: "Po' lil thang…she'd be better off dead."

"The blood was too strong for her all at once," Mama said. "It made her heart weak."

I lit out of the house so fast I didn't even put on my shoes. I ran all the way to the hospital. The nurse let me go into the room where they kept my sister. She had tubes running everywhere. Tubes up her nose. Tubes in her arms. Tubes in her ankles where the blood ran through her little body. She was in an oxygen tent and there was frost in her hair and eyebrows. Tears had frozen on her little face. She looked at me and opened her mouth, but no sound came out. I reached my hand into the tent and took her fingers into mine. I prayed hard to God to save her. I prayed all night long. I was still praying when I fell asleep. When we awoke the next morning, the nurses removed the oxygen tent. Felise was going to be all right.

So I had all this on my mind when I looked into her face as I boarded the bus. I guess that's what made me cry. I thought to myself, she's fine now. Grown and healthy and active. And the way she could eat, one would never know that anything was ever wrong.

We stopped to eat in Harrisburg, Pennsylvania. We sent a symbolic wave to the Steelers when we went through Pittsburgh. At the end of the second day we were in Chicago. There, we had a five hour layover. We marveled at the tall buildings and considered the notion of visiting the Sears Tower, but I didn't want to run the risk of missing our connection. So, the girls and I took turns washing up in the restroom and taking care of my son.

We arrived in Sacramento on the morning of the fourth day. My cousin's wife, Tammy, came to pick us up and drive us to Vacaville. Let me tell you…there has never been a more God forsaken place than Vacaville, California. I didn't say anything, of course, because I did not want to seem ungrateful. But Vacaville did not fit my image of California at all. I always thought about sunshine, orange trees and Disneyland when I thought about California. And people, too. Busy people. Busy living lives that were worth living. Things to do, places to see, the *let's do lunch* kind of thing.

But only three things were happening in Vacaville: Travis Air Force Base, where Rico was stationed, the correctional facility where they held Charles Manson, and the onion factory, which made Vacaville a kind of hamburger haven for motorists on the freeway. Everything else was tumble weeds with a few houses sprinkled in between. The closest store to buy milk or bread was a two mile walk along the railroad track.

We stayed there for three months. At first, I went out looking for a job every day. I went to San Francisco, Oakland and Sacramento, following leads from the newspaper and filling out applications for all kinds of positions. I had no training, couldn't type worth a quarter, and it was hard for me to accept the fact that nobody wanted to hire me just because I said I could learn quickly. I had been gainfully employed since I was seven years old, and I had not been denied a job in my whole life. It was 1982, and jobs were not easy to come by in a place that had little industry. Vacaville was very remote. The onion factory was not hiring, and the base had a long waiting list of potential civil servants. After the first month I resigned myself to the idea that perhaps I should write a book about my experiences with Hubbie. I was out of money by then, so when I enrolled the girls in school, one of the counselors advised me to go talk to the folks at Social Services.

My social worker took care of us immediately. She gave me food stamps and a check, and she enrolled my oldest daughter in a special school program for unwed mothers. The check wasn't much, but I gave half of it to Shug for rent and expenses. I tried to save some so we could get our own place, but the rent for a two bedroom apartment was over seven hundred dollars a month. My total income was less than three.

Shug's wife began to complain about us "sitting around" all day. She had every right to do that. My girls were not lazy, but they would not do a thing unless I told them to do it.

So there I was again living in someone else's house when I really was not welcome. I knew it. I could feel the tension whenever I tried to strike up a conversation with Tammy. I let it get to me, let it weigh on my mind. Hard as tried I could never save more than twenty or thirty dollars out of each check, and that just was not enough to get my own place. What made it so bad, Ronald was under court order to send me two hundred and fifty dollars a month for child support. When I moved to California he stopped sending payments. I am sure he was punishing me. He refused to send that money, or even acknowledge his son's birthday, for ten whole years. By the time the district attorney caught up with him he owed me more than twenty-six thousand dollars.

That is something I have never been able to understand. How can a man turn his back on his children simply because he doesn't get along with their mother? He knows that the child has to eat. The child needs shoes and clothes. But a man can walk away from his obligations to his child and still be a man. That's still a major problem in this country. Only recently have we begun to look at the situation from a different point of view and make men accountable for the children they sire. I know that there are some men who take care of their offspring as eagerly as the mothers do, but there are still too many men who don't. Once the relationship is over with the mother, they cut all ties to the whole family. They excuse themselves by saying that the women spend the money foolishly, and, let's face it, there are women who wear diamond studs in their ears when the kids are hungry and raggedy. But if that's the question, what's to stop him from buying the clothes and shoes and groceries himself? What's to stop him from taking the kid to a movie or the skating rink, or a ball game? And what, indeed, stops him from sending that child a birthday card with ten dollars in it to say, *Hey…I'm still your dad and if you need me just call?* It seems to me that when a woman opens her legs to receive a man she is taking on the responsibility of the entire human race. Man can simply walk away. When the child survives poverty, hunger and *fatherlessness,* when he becomes a famous ball player, or a teacher, or politician, or even if he just becomes a good man who respects and loves his own family, the father sticks out his chest and brags about *my son,* like he did something other than satisfy his biological needs.

The kids know that, too, without having to be told. Ever notice athletes on TV? When the camera focuses on them they always say, "Hi Mom." They never recognize their father unless they say, "Hi Mom and Dad." They put her first, see? I have seen fathers get pissed about that, let me tell you, but the fact is those young people remember who helped them get where they are. They remember who was there to feed them when they were hungry, nurse them when they were sick, make sacrifices and deny herself when they needed something *extra.*

As Edgar Allan Poe would say, "You, who so well know the nature of my soul…" must understand that I am not male-bashing here. I simply want to share with you my observations. If you are not guilty of this, you should have nothing to say. If you are guilty, sit down and shut up and *listen* to what I am trying to tell you. We are never going to correct this problem if we continue to refuse to hear each other. Those of us who have found ourselves in a desperate situation and have to accept welfare have often been labeled as "dysfunctional" by the working class. More often than not, the same people who slander us are responsible for our poverty. Just because a child does not live under your roof is no excuse for your failure to support him or her. But when you don't send the money, and the mother has to take welfare, you call her lazy and you are glad you got rid of her. It is a disease that spreads through every culture, but it is particularly visible in the black community. Every day I hear brothers talking about what the white man won't let them do. *The white man won't let me do this…the white man won't let me do that.* It's like a goddamned song. Then they turn right around and let the white man tell them when to feed their kids. This sickness needs to be cured. The children are the ones who suffer because of it.

nineteen

The lack of money was one of my biggest problems when I lived in Shug's house. The fact that my son was sick all the time was another one. The poor little guy had had pneumonia four times before he was a year old, and one day, when he started wheezing, I thought he had pneumonia again. When I took him to the doctor and had him ex-rayed, it turned out that he needed a *bronchoscopy* because apparently he had aspirated a peanut. I took him to Oakland's Children's Hospital. We arrived at four in the afternoon and the procedure was to be done at seven o'clock the next morning.

The first thing the hospital staff did wrong was to send a white-uniformed nurse into the baby's room. To him, the uniform meant needles. He cuddled close to me and watched the nurse out of the corner of his eye. He was only twenty months old and he still had the scars from the last series of shots. At that time they had plunged him into a bucket of ice water to break the fever, and he had to take four shots a day in each thigh (that's eight shots per day) for five days. His little legs looked like pin cushions, and he was not about to let this nurse touch him without a fight. So when she approached the bed to try to put a little bag on him so they could test his urine, he put up such a fuss that it took two grown orderlies and me to hold him.

He absolutely refused to pee in that bag. They kept checking on him every hour and, through the force of sheer will on that child's part, the bag remained dry. He stayed awake for hours, watching the white uniforms and cuddling close to me every time one of them entered the room.

When the shift changed at eleven that night, another nurse came into the room and began to hook up something that they were going to do intravenously. The child saw that and began to squirm. I told her that she would need some help because he was very strong. She did not take my word. When she tried to stick the needle in his arm, he uppercut her chin with his foot. They wrestled for a full minute. He kicked and screamed, "No! Nooooo!" I put my leg across his and held both his arms. The nurse managed to get the needle in place. The baby stopped crying and started coughing violently. It looked like he was gasping for air, so I said to the nurse: "He's not breathing."

112

"Of course he's breathing," she said. "It's just a temper tantrum. He's just spoiled."

I kept looking at my son and he looked...*different.* He was very still, and his eyes were wide open and unfocused, like he was staring at something and was surprised at what he saw. He didn't breathe at all, and I repeated to the nurse: "He's NOT breathing."

"Ma'am, the child is breathing and you're not helping here. Look at his stomach."

I looked at his stomach; it was flat and wrinkled, but there was no movement. Then, all of a sudden, he closed his eyes and turned a deep royal blue all over. I screamed, "Oh God! He's dead!"

With that another nurse came into the room and the first nurse told her, "Maybe you'd better get some help."

I won't lie. I lit up Children's Hospital that day. I ran down the hall screaming, "I told her he wasn't breathing. I told her!" Thirty or forty doctors and nurses ran past me in the direction of my son's room. I could hear that emergency buzzer: *blahmp...blahmp...* and the voice behind it: *code blue...code blue. Two, four, zero. Code blue.*

Two nurses chased me and tackled me to the floor. I said it over and over again, "I told her he wasn't breathing. I told her. Oh, God! Please don't let him die!"

The team of doctors and nurses worked on my child for what seemed like a long time. Finally, one of them came to me and said he was all right.

"We turned him over and whacked him on the back. A piece of the peanut came out. When he coughed, it apparently broke into little pieces and, *apparently,* one of them lodged in his windpipe."

"May I see him?"

"Yes, of course. We'll need to do the surgery right away, but first, I want to know what happened here."

The doctor led me to my son while I told him the story. I don't know what, if anything, they did to that crazy nurse, but I do know that when I reached my son, the pee bag was full.

❁   ❁   ❁

Trying to keep that child alive, trying to stretch my welfare check, trying to keep the girls in school, off drugs, and out of gangs kept me half crazy myself. As I said before, it weighed me down and kept me from thinking clearly. One day, after I had cooked dinner for my own children, I realized that I needed to cook something for Shug's son. He didn't eat boiled vegetables, so I had to prepare something different for him. I decided to fry some shrimp, and just as I put the frying pan on the stove, I heard the baby stir from his nap. I went in to check on him. He needed a change and a bath, so I did all that while I was with him in the back of the house. When I started down the hallway towards the kitchen, I noticed that the house was filled with black smoke. I had forgotten about the pan of grease on the stove. I grabbed my son and ran to a neighbor's house to call the fire department. They came right away, but the fire had almost completely destroyed the kitchen.

That was probably the worst day of my life. Shug had been good to me and my family. I repaid him by nearly burning down his house. He came in from work that day and said, "Barbr'ann, what happened?" And even though I told him the story, I could not forgive myself for the fire. I wore that burden in my heart and my head like a heavy cloud, and for the rest of my stay there, I could not look Shug in the eye.

The shit kept getting more and more ragged. Tammy was upset because my kids took their orders from me, not her. We all reached the point where we didn't want to go to the house. We just stayed away all day long and only went there to sleep. When Shug and his family had had enough of us, he didn't tell me to get out, but what he did say made me leave. He said, "There is only one boss in this house, and that's Tammy. If you can't do what she tells you to do, you have an option."

That made sense. It was her house. But she was five years younger than I and I wasn't about to let her tell me what to do. So I left. The only problem was that I had just given them my rent money and I was almost broke. After I bought the bus tickets I had sixty-eight dollars left. Still, we packed our stuff, got on that Greyhound and headed for Los Angeles.

twenty

Now. Los Angeles was where I wanted to get in the first place. When we arrived there on November 21, 1982, I only had forty-two dollars to my name. I didn't know anyone in L.A., but I had a phone number of a long-ago friend who lived in Inglewood. I had not seen her in twenty years. Sylvia Miller, her name was in high school. Sylvia Anderson, now. She was the daughter of my favorite teacher when I was a teenager in Wilson. Sylvia, herself, was a teacher now and she taught English and drama in one of the high schools in L.A. Unified. I had called her once to ask about the job situation there. I even wrote a letter to Mayor Tom Bradley, but he never answered. So when I got to L. A., the first thing I did was call Sylvia. She told me to stay put and she would make some calls to find me a place to stay. I gave her the number of the pay phone (that was when you could still call a pay phone in L. A.), and we waited for her to call back.

We stayed at the Union Bus Station for several hours. Finally, Sylvia called and said that someone from the Narcotics Squad would pick us up and take us to the YMCA in Hollywood. Hollywood! How exciting it all seemed.

Detective Waters or Watson, or something with a W showed up with his partner in a Granada. We had seven trunks. He managed to get all of that and us into or onto that little vehicle. He drove the scenic route, showed us all of downtown, took us on the "strip" on Sunset Blvd., and promised us that if he ever caught one of us on that little stretch, he'd run us in without question.

We checked into the Y and paid the guy at the desk twenty-two dollars. My son was sick again. He kept throwing up and he had difficulty breathing. I didn't know what was wrong with him this time. He stayed awake all night long, crawling back and forth on the bed. He said things that broke my heart: "Help me. Help me please." All I could do was hold him in my arms.

We had to be out of the Y by eight the next morning. The guy at the desk let me leave my trunks there in storage until I could find a place to live. He said I should try the Salvation Army on Ninth and Figueroa, and then he pointed to Children's Hospital on Sunset.

I bought breakfast for the kids and, after they ate, we took a city bus down to Children's Hospital. The doctor said that my son was having an asthma attack. I never knew he had asthma. It took four shots of adrenaline at twenty-minute intervals to bring him out of it. It must have been pretty awful for him because he didn't even protest when he saw the needles coming. In fact, he seemed to welcome them.

With that crisis over I called the Salvation Army and told Rachel, the receptionist, my situation. She told me how to get there. We went back to the Y and got those seven trunks, caught a bus at the corner and loaded them. I did not have enough money for bus fare; I only had a dollar and nineteen cents. When I told the driver where I was going, he let us ride free.

When I look back on that day now, it all seems so strange to me, almost funny. People say that big cities are cold. Even Miss Louise had told me, "Don't let them city slickers slick you." But I had already found more warmth and understanding in Los Angeles than I ever thought possible. When I say "funny," I don't mean laughing funny. I mean, we didn't know that city or any of its dangers, but it just felt right.

We certainly didn't know the streets at all, or even how to ride RTD. So, when we got to Ninth and Figueroa, we didn't have sense enough to pull the string and get off the bus. We got off at Olympic, which was actually Tenth street, but if you know anything at all about big cities, you know that was three blocks away from our destination. Naturally the driver was not going to turn around just for us, so we had to unload and carry the seven trunks three blocks back and one block up to get to the Salvation Army Shelter. My older daughter and I took one trunk to the end of the block while the younger one stayed with the baby. She stayed with that trunk while I went back and got the baby. I left my son with her while my younger daughter and I brought down another trunk. We kept repeating that pattern until we finally reached the mission. I was never so glad to see a bunk bed in all my days.

Our room had four beds and a bathroom. These were the rules: Lights out at ten p.m. Breakfast at six a.m., lunch at eleven, dinner at five. The rent was twenty-two dollars a night. No social drugs were allowed. Prescription medicines had to be left at Linda's office to be distributed by her. The adult tenant had to apply for welfare if he/she had no money, and that person had to look for work every day. No fighting. No guests. The maximum stay was two weeks.

We, however, stayed at the mission for three weeks. That was mostly be-cause we were what they considered to be a "model" family. The kids and I bathed everyday, brushed our teeth and prayed before we ate—that kind of thing. So when Rachael asked me to talk with a reporter for the Associated Press, I said, "Sure." I saw that as an opportunity to let all of Los Angeles know that I was looking for work.

The reporter and her cameraman came into our little room and, while she and I talked, he took dozens of pictures. She asked me questions about Wilson, why I chose Los Angeles, what I planned to do with the rest of my life. I answered her thoroughly and intelligently. Let me assure you of that. She asked me, "Don't you think it was rather naïve of you to bring three children all the way across the country when you knew you did not have a job?"

I gave her one of those "I-don't-believe-you!" looks just as the cameraman snapped the picture. I said, "You may call it naïve, but I call it gutsy. I was not happy where I was. I think I deserve happiness, don't you?"

When she said, "Hmmm," and turned her mouth upside down, I decided not to pursue the issue. We had talked for over two hours and she seemed to be writing down every word.

"What do you plan to do with this information?" I wanted to know.

"I'm going to write an article about you."

"Where will you print it?"

"Oh…it'll be in every major newspaper in this country."

"Well, I'd like to make a request. I do not want it to go to *The Wilson Daily Times*. Folks back there won't understand that I am actually doing okay."

"Fine. No problem."

Wouldn't you know? *Wilson Daily Times* was the first to publish that article. That "I-don't-believe-you!" picture was splattered all over the front page. And the only "writing" was the caption: *This Fatherless Family Will Spend Christmas at a Los Angeles County Mission*. There was no mention whatsoever of my dreams, my goals, my ambitions or my plans. There was just a pitiful looking picture with that nasty title under it.

I knew what would happen next and I was prepared for it. Some folks in Wilson laughed. They thought I finally had gotten what I deserved. *The bitch done broke two good men. It's time for her to suffer a little bit*. Some felt sorry for me. *Poor thang. Never could be satisfied. Cut off her own nose to spite her face*. Then there were those who really cared about what happened to me. Mrs. Estelle Coble, Maurice's mother, wrote me a letter: *Women like you add new dimension to the phrase, "Yes, I can!"* And Mr. Fitch, who used to be the mailman when I was a kid and understood my hurt every time he didn't bring me a letter from Pop, offered to pay my way back home.

For that I was and am forever grateful, but I didn't want to go back to Wilson. I was already "home." Even though I was in transit and had already left the Salvation Army, I knew in my heart that Los Angeles was where I belonged. Robert Frost once wrote: "Home is a place where, when you have to go there, they have to take you in." Los Angeles took me in and re-raised me, nurtured me and gave me a chance to be me. It had that feeling, you know, of *home*.

twenty-one

Except the Lord keep the city, the watchman waketh but in vain.
—Psalms 127:1

One of the counselors at the mission had a house for rent. She was a large Mexican woman who looked Samoan. Her name was Bonnie, and she said, "I have a three-bedroom house on London Street in Hollywood. $450 a month. It's yours if you want it, Hon." I took the house sight unseen and gave Bonnie all the money I had as a down payment. Forty dollars. The kids and I moved in on the evening of December 10, 1982. There was another family already living in the house, a fact that Bonnie neglected to share with me. Mr. Sanchez had six children—five sons and a daughter—and they used the two front bedrooms. Bonnie escorted me to the back bedroom where there was a mattress and a box spring. The baby and I slept on the mattress. My older daughter slept on the box spring, and the other child slept on the floor. There was one bathroom and one kitchen in the house, a small living room and a dining area. There was a washing machine. The clothesline was in the backyard.

I asked her about Mr. Sanchez. "How long will he be here?"

"As long as it takes, Hon."

"What do you mean?"

"His wife left him with those children. He needs a place to live."

"But I thought I was renting the whole house."

She looked at me as if I had said that Jesus wore pink panties. "Really, Hon? Surely you don't expect to rent a house of this quality for $450 a month!"

"Well, how much is the rent?"

"Twelve hundred, Hon." She said that with such a matter-of-factness, that the shock didn't register until years later. "You can't afford that. But even if you could, what would we do with poor Mr. Sanchez, Hon?"

Of course, I wasn't the least bit worried about "poor Mr. Sanchez," but I was concerned about my own children and how I was going to pay the balance of the rent. There was something else, too. Neither Mr. Sanchez nor I had keys to the house. Bonnie kept them, and she entered the house at will. She'd come over at six o'clock every morning and do her laundry. Or, she'd just make us all get up. Sometimes she would just sit at the table and talk on the phone. On occasion I caught her going through our things. She spoke to Mr. Sanchez in Spanish, and though I did not really understand the language and could only decipher words like *dinero* and *nada,* and *caca,* I understood the look. She told him that I had only given her forty dollars.

On Saturday before Christmas Bonnie took me to Our Lady of Laredo Catholic Church and introduced me to Monsignor John P. Languille. He was the one who helped me get started in Los Angeles.

There was another church that helped us, too. It was The New Commandment Church in Paramount. Reverend and Mrs. Grady Jones used to drive to Hollywood every Sunday morning to pick us up and take us to Sunday School and Church. Afterwards they'd give us dinner and take us home with enough grocery money to last for a week. Or, they'd go into their own freezer and pull out meat and vegetables for us. I saw them as good, Christian-hearted people.

Monsignor told me to go find a decent place to live, and once that was accomplished, he gave me the money for my first apartment. I chose a place that was at the foot of Queen of Angels Hospital. My apartment was on the third floor and it overlooked the Hollywood Freeway. I remember praying for four walls and a roof, and that was pretty much all I got. There was a stove, refrigerator and a dishwasher, but I didn't have a stick of furniture. For the first few weeks we slept and ate on the floor. We used our coats for blankets and our sweaters for pillows. But thanks to John (he insisted that I call him that), we did at least have shelter and food, and for that, too, I am grateful.

Oh, there were plenty of times when we did not have what we wanted to eat. In the lobby of Social Services, for example, there was a vendor who sold hot dogs for a dollar and twenty-nine cents, and I didn't have a dollar and twenty-nine cents. We did, however, have food at home. I remember a time when my brother said, "Mama, I'm *hongry,*" and I watched the tears well up in her eyes. My kids have never been *hongry.* I have been blessed that way. There is a huge difference between hungry and *hongry.* When you are hungry you're ready to eat, and you know there is something there for you. When you are *hongry,* you don't know when you are going to eat again. You don't know where the food is; you have to go find it.

I wanted to make sure that my kids never experienced the kind of hunger my brother and I knew. Aside from stealing pecans from The Satchells, we also stole peaches, apples and purple plums. The plums were my favorites, and it was the plums that made the Satchells my favorite neighbors to rob. Whenever we knew they were not at home, Jr. and I would hop the fence and steal the plums. Jr. liked the ripe ones, the ones that had fallen to the ground. I liked to eat the green ones and put salt on them. Now, that was some good eating, even though I knew I'd have a bellyache by the time Mama got home. She used to think I was puny because I had so many bellyaches.

Mama worked from can't see in the morning to can't see at night, but on Saturdays she'd get off at noon. Saturdays were the best. Mama would order groceries and send them home in a taxi. Jr. and I would put the stuff away and then make us some sandwiches. We could make some sandwiches! Bologna. Sausage. Peanut butter and banana. We'd make sandwiches piled two inches high, sometimes with three pieces of bread. Then we'd mash them down and go sit on the back porch, swinging our legs and giggling over our fortune. We used to take a bite and then look at that sandwich, talk to it, sing to it, laugh at it and try to figure out where we would hit it next. I always ate mine from the top to the bottom. I'd take a big bite out of the middle, hit again on the left and then on the right to make it even. Jr. started at the bottom and ate all around the crust until he only had a circle left. Then he'd pop the whole thing in his mouth at one time.

Sandwich making was our forte. We ate up all the good stuff on Saturday, and the rest of the week we made mustard sandwiches, mayonnaise sandwiches, barbeque sauce sandwiches. A biscuit leftover from breakfast, a saucer full of molasses and a jelly jar filled with cold water were special, energizing treats for us. Every once in a while we'd find a leftover piece of fatback and, after eating the meat, we'd hold the skin between our cheek and gums for hours.

We were lucky. We could always *find* something to eat. After all, we did have the Satchells' backyard. But that's not the kind of lesson you can pass on. California had beautiful trees, too, but if you hop a fence to steal fruit there, you're likely to get shot. So, I am grateful that my kids have never had to go find something to eat. The Joneses saw to that. We ate Christmas dinner with them and, thanks to them and John, the baby had plenty of presents.

And John had plenty of connections. At the beginning of 1983, I asked him if he would vouch for me to get some furniture from St. Vincent de Paul's Thrift Shop. I promised to pay fifty dollars a month. He agreed. On January 2, we all went shopping at Kmart for our monthly supplies. On our way home we stopped at Londondale Fish and Chips at the corner of Beverly and 11th Street. There was a man standing outside the restaurant who reminded me of Moses. He wore a long over-sized coat, a scraggly beard and he was holding a Bible. The people inside the store were laughing at him. I fed my children and, since we all had bus transfers to get us home, I gave that man the two dollars I had left. The bus came and we boarded. Once seated, I turned to observe the man enjoying the food he had ordered. It gave me such a good feeling to be able to help someone else.

The next morning I left the children at home while I traveled the hour-long bus ride to St. Vincent de Paul. When I got off the bus and crossed the street, there was a construction site with a chain-link fence surrounding it. Two dollars rolled along the fence, and when I picked it up, I believed it was God's way of showing me that I had done some good the previous night.

I walked into the store and was greeted by a man named Alex. He walked me through the store as I picked out two beds, a sofa bed, a re-cliner, a stereo, pots, pans, dishes and utensils, a dining set with four chairs, a couple of lamps, a television and a set of Funk and Wagnall. The bill came to over four hundred dollars. I told him that Monsignor wanted him to call and I gave him the number to John's direct line.

"I'm not going to call him. You call him. There's a pay phone right out there in the hall."

I went to the pay phone and called John's number. He said, "Let me speak with Alex."

Of course, I could only hear Alex's end of that conversation, but I noticed that he exhibited a rainbow of colors—red, purple, green—during that brief encounter and he started to sweat: "Yes, Monsignor. Of course, Sir. Oh, yes, Sir, I love my job. Right away, Monsignor. Absolutely. No. No. No problem, Sir."

Alex was wiping his brow and shaking his head when he returned the phone to me. I said, "Hello?" and John said, "Happy Birthday, Darling."

It was an early birthday present, surely. My birthday was two months away, but when I got home, the furniture was there, everything was in place and the kids were watching TV.

❁   ❁   ❁

John sent me to several places during my job search and he always called before I got there. The first place he sent me to was the Employment Development Department. The administrator there gave me a typing test. I knew I couldn't type, but I tried anyway. So when the score came back at forty-three words a minute, this strange- looking guy called me to his cubicle. By *strange* I mean I am accustomed to interviewers being neatly dressed and well-groomed, at least a tie. This guy was dirty. He was tall and very white.

He wore a shirt that was missing a button, and his collar lay open so you could see the ring. His thin, brownish-gray hair went every which way and he kept scratching his head. He had a huge belly, and he kept lighting a new cigarette with the one he had just finished. He fumbled over some papers for a minute and then he said, "Ya did well, but ya didn't pass."

"I never was any good at typing," I said.

"Can ya drive?"

"Yes!"

"Good. I have something here as a driver for a Pizza company. Ya got a car?"

"No."

"Hmmm. Can ya work a switchboard?"

"I don't know. Why?"

"There's a position as a receptionist—"

"Okay, look. I need a job. I can worry about a *position* later."

He put the papers aside then. "Well, what d'ya wanna do?"

"Listen," I said. "I can do anything. I'm willing to do anything. I have three kids to feed." I was thinking about scrubbing toilets, mopping floors, any kind of honest work. The smirk on his face told me that they already had enough people doing that, and I could see he had obviously lost patience with me.

"Well, if I find anything like that I'll letcha know. In the meantime, don't go around telling people thatcha can do anything."

"Why not?"

"Because there are a lot of things thatcha can't do. I mean, ya can't be a nuclear physicist." He laughed then and his nose whistled while the hairs in it flopped back and forth.

I didn't like that at all. People in authority are always judging. I could be a nuclear physicist if I wanted to be one. I'd have to get some education, but I could do it if I wanted to. I found myself whining a little bit when I left that office. *I could do it; I just don't want to.*

The second place John sent me to caused another permanent change in my life. Not the place itself, but the things that happened as a result of me being there. It was The United Way. Again, I had to take a typing test that I failed. You need to know ahead of time that telling you this part frightens me. It makes me weak and vulnerable. I need you to concentrate on how you would feel if it happened to you. Shift your focus away from me and realize that things like this do happen much too often. I buried it way down into the inside part of me and left it there for years. That way I didn't have to deal with it, or think about it, and it started to seem like a dream, a nightmare. For a long time it seemed like I had heard it secondhand, like it had happened to someone else in a far off distant place. But there came a time when I had to think about and act on it. I had to bring the inside to the outside.

If it looks like I am giving you a *just the facts Ma'am* account of these events, understand that it is sooooo hard. I am afraid that you will blame me. If you have to do that I'll accept it, but I want you to understand my weakness and forgive my stupidity. Know that there is nothing you can say to me or about me that I have not already said to myself. It still makes me blue.

The place was the United Way. When I arrived there a tall, handsome Black man greeted me at the door. He seemed glad to see me, and after looking around for a few minutes I realized why. He and I were the only color. He pushed a broom, but I noticed that he stayed close to the testing area. He watched me continuously, protectively. After I failed the test and was about to leave, he asked my name, where I was from, how long I had been in L. A., and how about lunch sometime.

"Sure," I said.

"How 'bout today?" he said. "My name is Henry."

"What time?"

"How 'bout one o'clock?"

"Okay."

"Do you like fish?"

I liked fish, so I gave him my address and we agreed to meet at my apartment.

One o'clock came and went. At two o'clock I made lunch for the kids and myself. About three o'clock Bert and Marge, a couple I had met at the mission, stopped by to see how I was doing. We talked for a while. At four o'clock Henry showed up, loaded down with a big greasy bag full of fish. I explained to him that we had already eaten, so Bert and Marge ate the fish and then they left.

Henry stayed for a long time. He was in my way a little, but my home training wouldn't allow me to be rude to him. I listened to him ramble on and on about his life, his family, his plans to start a business.

At about seven o'clock in the evening, my son started to wheeze. I panicked. We were a long way from Children's Hospital and I didn't have bus fare. Henry offered to drive us and wait until the baby was better.

It was January 4, 1983.

By the time we got back to my apartment it was well past midnight. The girls were asleep. I put the baby to bed and closed the bedroom door. I offered Henry some coffee, which he declined, and then he left, saying that he had to be at work by six in the morning.

Fifteen minutes later, Henry came back. "Well, this is embarrassing," he said. "My car won't start. I think I have a problem with the ignition. It does that from time to time. All I have to do is wait a few hours and it will start." He looked around the living room. "Do you mind if I just sorta bunk out on this recliner and leave for work in the morning?"

I saw no great problem with that since he had been so good about getting my son to and from the hospital. So I gave him a blanket and I stretched out, fully dressed, on the sofa bed.

I woke up at exactly one o'clock. Henry was on top of me. I made a noise, a scream, maybe, and pushed against his chest with both hands. He covered my mouth with one hand and held my shoulder with the other. I crossed my legs at the knees and mumbled my protest under the weight of his hand. We wrestled for what seemed like a long time and all the while he was talking to me: "Don't fight it. You know you want it. If you scream your kids will hear you."

All kinds of things went through my mind. I did not want to frighten my children, but I was determined to fight him. I kept my knees locked. I hit him on his head and across his back. I bit his fingers. He seemed to enjoy that, and he was just as determined as I. He managed to get his knee between mine. He put his hand under my dress and ripped away my panties.

"Hey…take it easy," he said. "It'll be all over soon. I won't hurt you. You don't want to wake up your children, do you?"

He was right. It was all over very soon. When he finished, he got up and left. He never even took off his shoes.

I went to check on the kids. They were fast asleep. I was confused. On the one hand I felt like Henry had taken away the only thing I had left that was truly mine. On the other hand, after the way I had behaved with Ronald while I was still married to Hubbie, I figured I deserved it. It was my punishment. Payback. I had lived the life of a tramp so it was only fitting that my body should be accessible to everyone. I decided that it was no great big deal and I gave myself some old advice: *You can't miss what you can't measure.* I wasn't cut, bleeding, strangled or dead. This was an isolated incident, and nobody had to know.

twenty-two

I kept that secret from my children. They trusted me to make things right for them and I couldn't let them know that I had faltered. I put it all in the back of my mind and determined to move forward. It looked like I was not going to find a job until I got some training, so I went to Los Angeles City College and registered for some courses.

I was thirty-seven years old, and it seemed a little weird to be in college. I had heard, though, that folks older than I went back to school, and as long as my brain still worked I figured I should be okay. I had to take some placement exams, apply for a Pell Grant and stand in some pretty long lines. But since I was on welfare, I did not have to pay tuition, and that made things possible for me. I knew it would not be easy; possible is what I prayed for. If God would make it possible, I could do the rest.

While I was standing in one of those lines at L.A.C.C., I had a chance to talk with some of the returning students. We were all busy making plans for our futures and, occasionally, we'd sit down to talk over a cup of coffee and a sandwich. Registration took about a week. During this time we became a group—a unit, you might say—that looked out for each other and shared information about classes, teachers, used books and the like. One of the guys in our group was a young African from Nigeria. He had fascinating stories about his culture, his country, his tribe. One day a white girl in our group asked him if they wore clothes in Africa. He said, "Oh no! We wear fig leaves and ostrich feathers!" Then he winked at me. At the time, there was not a whole lot of humor in my life, but that was funny. I laughed until I cried.

His name was Kwame, and his last name was so long that I never could pronounce it properly. He quickly became my favorite person in the group. I felt comfortable with him. He was short and small framed—not the least bit threatening. On the last day of registration, he offered me a ride home and I accepted it eagerly. I had been standing on the corner of Vermont and Melrose shifting from foot to foot trying to decide which way I should go home. I had just enough bus fare to make the full trip—fifty cents for the first ride and a dime for the transfer. (In those days, you could use one

126

transfer all day long.) If I caught the east bound #10 at Melrose and Vermont, I'd have to walk six blocks to get home. If I caught the southbound #11, I'd still have to walk the six blocks, but I would have a transfer, which meant that I would be completely broke, but the #11 would come sooner than the #10.

So as I stood there trying to figure out the best route, Kwame stopped at the light in his white Mustang.

"Where are you going?"

"Home."

"Where is that?"

"Over by Queen of Angels."

"Want a ride?"

"Sure!"

I hopped into his car without thinking about anything beyond saving my last sixty cents. He took me straight home.

A few days later I was on my way to the corner store when I saw Kwame drive by. I waved. He stopped. He gave me a lift again. He took me to the store and back home. Then he asked me if I wanted to go for a ride. "I'll show you the city," he said. I agreed to go, so we dropped the groceries off at my place and then we left.

At the time it looked like we actually did go for a ride. As I sit here and remember it, though, I can see that he took me straight to his apartment. Indeed he pointed out things along the way—the La Brea Tar Pits, famous restaurants and museums that made it look like a tour. After I got to know the city, however, I realized that he took the shortest route possible to his place.

He said, "Come on in for a minute. I need to pick up something, and I want you to see how I decorated my apartment."

I went in and sat down. His little spot was very nice. African masks and other artifacts all over the walls. A zebra-like rug. Glass tables. Light brown furniture. I felt a little ill at ease, but I was not worried. He was such a little guy.

Kwame poured a glass of wine for me and sat a cold beer next to it. I passed on the beer, but I took a sip of the wine. He put on some music and asked me to dance.

"I don't dance," I told him and kept my seat. "I really should be getting back to the kids."

"You mean you don't like to dance?"

"I mean I don't know how." I explained that Ronald was a great dancer, but the best I could do was shake my booty.

"Oh, come on. I'll teach you." With that he started snapping his fingers and wiggling his butt. He looked rather ridiculous, actually, but I guessed that it was the way they danced in Africa. I laughed, and I could feel myself relaxing a bit. I stood up and said, "Okay."

He never taught me one step. Rather, he picked me up and practically ran to the bedroom. That's what I get for under-estimating a little man. He dumped me on the bed and hopped on top of me. It all happened so fast. I remember saying to him, "Wait. Wait a minute. You can't do this to me!" I remember that I slapped him. I remember that he slapped me back. And I remember the moment of surrender. I thought about Miss Louise: *Don't let them city slickers slick you.* I thought about Hubbie, Ronald, Henry, Monsignor, the police. I thought about my daughters and how I had broken every rule I ever set for them: *Always take your purse. Take your own money. Don't let a man take advantage of you. Make sure I know where you are at all times. Never, ever get in a car with someone I don't know.*

Yes, I thought about my children. They had no idea where I was. I had no idea where I was. I had left my apartment without my purse, so I had no identification on me. He could kill me and no one would ever find me. That was the moment of surrender. I stopped fighting and let him have his way.

Afterwards we both cried. "I can't believe I did that," he said. It was January 12, 1983.

twenty-three

My period was due on January 19 at three o'clock in the afternoon. It did not come. I didn't panic. I thought about Hubbie's mother who had given birth to fifteen children. She said that every time she missed a period her husband would say that maybe she had a cold. Her most famous line was, "I had fifteen goddamned colds and now they all have colds of their own!"

In early February I went to the doctor who confirmed that I was pregnant. I walked from that office in a daze. I saw it as a punishment for that abortion. It was as if God was saying, "Look. I want you to have four kids. If you get rid of this one I'll give you another one. Now. What are you going to do?"

I lived in anguish during the next few days. I had no one I could talk to and expect to understand or help. I was embarrassed about what had happened, and I was ashamed that it had happened to me. I called my mother. I figured I should go on and "fess up" because it wasn't exactly the kind of secret that would keep. I said to her, "I don't know what's going on in my old age. Looks like every time I turn around I'm getting knocked up." My mother, in all her infinite wisdom, said to me, "Well, Honey, stop turning around."

I laughed at that, but after a while it made perfect sense. I had been going round and round in circles, playing the role of victim. I had not moved forward one little bit; still, I refused to go backward. I took a long, hard look at my life and I discovered that I was my worst enemy. I kept doing things that defeated my purpose. That was something I could change. All I had to do was figure out how.

Changing your life is a difficult task, but only because of the "how." It is more than just a notion. You have to have a plan. I looked inside myself and realized that changes had to be made. I even knew what was wrong, but how to do it was the challenge. It was not going to happen overnight, I knew that. As a matter of fact, it happened so gradually that I didn't even notice it until it was done. Then one day I looked into the mirror and said to myself: "Hey…this is me! This is who I am!" But before I got there I had to pay some dues. I had to sing the blues. I had to break some rules and move on.

We talked about that before, breaking the rules, I mean. I broke just about all of them. Man's law would let me abort a child that was conceived in rape, but I reflected on the abortion I'd had earlier and I decided that I could not go through that hell again.

Then two things happened that turned out to be the best I could have done for myself during this that time. First, I read Maya Angelou's book, *I Know Why the Caged Bird Sings.* That book changed my way of thinking. It reminded me that I was not the only Black woman in the world who had to go through hard times. It taught me how to forgive myself for the things I did that everybody else thought were wrong. It allowed me to see that nothing would just come my way; I had to get out there and make things happen.

The second thing I did was talk to John. Of course, I had to hear a long lecture about putting myself into dangerous situations, and he said, "Darling I am disappointed that you've been involved with someone else since we met," but he promised to take care of me until the baby was born.

He kept that promise. Hardly a day went by that he didn't call me, and I saw him two, maybe three times a week. He never insisted on converting me to Catholic, never tried to force me to go to church. He seemed to be happy with me just as I was. I could count on him for anything. If I needed money, he'd give me cash from his personal fund. If I needed more than what he had, he'd take me to his office at Catholic Charities and get the money there. He offered to put my kids in Catholic School, and he used his influence all over town to make sure that I was comfortable.

John's plan, *hope,* was for me to give up the child for adoption. I already knew that I would not do that and I told him so. If I were going to birth a baby I was going to keep a baby. There was no question about it.

I thought about the women I knew in the pre-birth control era, and I realized that they had set an example for me. Aunt Flora and Aunt Doretta had both given birth to twelve children. They worked every day, stopping just long enough to push out another child. They made no excuses. Aunt Flora was a seamstress and she worked at home. Many a day I have seen her pedaling that sewing machine while one of those babies sucked on her breast and another pulled furiously on a sugar tit.

Aunt Doretta worked in service and she earned twelve dollars a week. Her husband died young and left her with all those kids. She worked hard to feed and educate them. Sometimes she'd walk to work. Sometimes her white lady would chauffer her in the back seat of the family car. She worked all day long cooking, cleaning, babysitting and keeping things in order for her white folks. Then she'd come home at night and do the same thing for her own family. I don't think I ever saw her without an apron.

It occurred to me that the things my mother and her sisters had to deal with made my little problems look like nothing. They had to scrub somebody else's floors down on their knees, clean somebody else's filth with their bare hands, cook somebody else's food. They stared heartache in the face and fought back with their dignity. They had to say "Yes Suh" to ten year old boys. They had to say "Miss Lucy" when they talked to three year old girls. They had to grin and bear it when the boss lady called them "colored girls" even when they had grown children and grandchildren.

Quiet as it's kept, they took shit off their men, too. I'm talking about real women—Aunt Flora, Aunt Doretta, Aunt Aileen, Aunt Minnie Bell, Mama—women who took whatever came their way and dealt with it the best they could. Women who greeted life's disappointments as tests of their own strength. Women who kneaded life with their hands, carried it on their backs, wore it under their hearts. They wrung out so much laundry... their fingers forgot to uncurl. I'm talking about women whose horizons were always within walking distance. Women who wore their sweat like a crowning glory. They snatched out an offensive tooth in the blink of an eye. Soothed their varicose veins, thick as fingers, and kept on going. I'm talking about women who would save you the heart of a watermelon and then tear your ass up for eating it before supper. They could make a pot of black-eyed peas taste like Christmas. They had no idea what it meant to be a "housewife;" work and sacrifice were all they knew. And the good news was that I was lucky enough to have been in their company when I was a child. Watching them, the real women, and remembering how they used to handle things gave me courage to keep pushing. That, coupled with Angelou's book, made me declare: *victim no more!*

If the truth be told, it was Aunt Doretta alone who recognized and encouraged the rebel in me. She once told me, "You be true to yourself. Don't ever stop fighting and don't you ever let anybody change who you are." She did not have a lot of education, but she was heavily gifted with mother wit. What she said made sense. I really wanted to run away, I'll admit that. I wanted to take flight and leave again, but I sensed that I would be giving someone else too much power. I was a thirty-seven year old runaway with three kids. Now I was pregnant again and I didn't even know who had done it. Kwame and Henry had taken something away from me. The man at the employment office had taken something away from me. The pregnancy was taking something away from me, but I was not going down without a fight. Perhaps I'd have to put my dreams on hold for a while, but I would not surrender. Ever.

twenty-four

I dropped all my classes except Creative Writing. This would be my last child; I signed the papers to shut down the baby factory. All I had to do was wait until that child started school, just four short years, then I could go back to college.

It was a good plan and I followed it, but all kinds of things started to happen that let me know how the system works against poor people. I will not try to tell you everything, but there are a couple of things I need to mention so you can see how poverty induces vulnerability and corruption.

A letter came in the mail from a man in Plano, Texas. It had been opened and forwarded to me. Inside there was a money order for thirteen dollars and a short, hand-written note that read, "For lunch and bus fare today." The man had signed his name and put his phone number at the bottom. I called to thank him for the money and, when he found out that the money order was the first thing I had received from him he broke down and cried.

"Oh Lord, Barbara," he said. "I'm not a rich man. I works ever'day. I sent you three hundred and eighty-two dollars since I seen your picture in the paper."

I was shocked to hear that news. The thirteen dollars was all I got, but I assumed that since I had been in transit for a while, maybe it was just held up in the mail. "Where did you send it?" I asked him.

"I sent the first couple hundred to the Salvation Army, but when I called and asked to speak to you they gave me an address on London Street and that's where I sent the rest."

"I only stayed there for a few weeks," I told him. "Maybe you can put a trace on the money orders."

"I sent cash. Special Delivery. Guess that wasn't too bright—"

I was inclined to agree with him, but I could tell that he was in pain. And I was getting hot. I remembered how Bonnie used to open Mr. Sanchez's mail and remove the cash. She told me that he could not read, so he had given her permission to handle his finances. I could hear the man from Texas talking, but nothing registered because I felt my blood pressure rising. It was evident that the counselors or someone at the mission, probably Bonnie, had taken the cash. The only reason I got the money order was that she could not cash it. She had sent it on to me thinking, I'm sure, that I would never find out about that other.

"—I ain't the smartest man in the worl'. And I ain't no pretty boy, neither. But I'm in love wif you, and I just wanted to help out. I sent you some flowers today to say so."

I thanked the man and promised to find out what happened to the money and the flowers. I gave him my address and phone number. I did not tell him I was pregnant.

After I hung up the phone, I hopped a bus and went to the house on London Street. Bonnie was at work and her daughter greeted me at the door. She said that some flowers had come but she didn't know what her mother had done with them. So I went to a phone booth and called Bonnie at the mission.

"What flowers, Hon?"

"The ones the man from Texas sent me."

"I don't know anything about any flowers, Hon."

To me this was proof that she deliberately stole from me. "Bonnie…" I said. "I've already been to your house. I spoke with your daughter. She said that you put the flowers away."

There was a long pause. Finally, Bonnie said, "Oh, *those* flowers. Yes. I put them in the back bedroom behind the door."

During the course of my life I have often wondered *why me?* I saw those times as moments of weakness. Now. I believe there is a reason for everything, and I have come to accept the fact that a part of my mission in this world is to observe and report certain violations against humanity. Catholic Charities, The Salvation Army, Goodwill the welfare system and the like are all programs that are designed to help people in need. But there is at least one person in every unit who works against the integrity of those programs. That person makes vulgar everything that is meant to help the poverty stricken. I have seen them in action. The employees of these institutions get theirs first. When they go to pick up donations, they sort through the items and pick out what they want before they deliver the rest to the store. Those charities, in turn, charge outrageous prices for the things the public has given them. Two hundred and twenty-five dollars for a used sofa might not seem like a lot, but for someone whose total income is less than six hundred a month, and there is no layaway plan, that is outrageous. The folks who can afford to shop from these places are folks who have good jobs and are looking for a bargain, not the people who really need the stuff.

Then there are all these "easy credit" places that sell *disposable* furniture. I call it disposable because once you finish paying for it, if you ever do, it's ready for the trash pile. That's right. You go into these places and they have pretty little trinkets carefully placed to make it all look good. You end of buying a dinette set for say, $399, and you set it up on a payment plan for ten dollars a week. Since you are on welfare, and they know that, you can go in on the first of the month and cash your check and make your payment for the entire month all in one stroke. They are glad to see you coming. They call you by your first name. But a year later, when the product breaks; when a leg falls off or the particle board cracks, they won't fix it or replace it because you or your children have "mishandled" the merchandise. They sympathize with you, of course, but you should have read the contract. They would like to sell you another one, a better one that is manufactured by this new company that stands behind its product, only you can't do that right now because you still owe $750 on this. So you're stuck with a piece of shit that you can't use but you still have to pay for.

Poor people are victimized by discrimination in this country more than any other group. Right now, if you have money, you can buy a car with no money down and 0% interest rate. If you are broke, however, you need two thousand dollars to get financed at 18%. The way the sales pitch sounds, "only 18%," makes you think you are getting a really good deal. You can buy a house with no down payment. Just before you sign the contracts you learn that "no down payment" means you have to come up with $7500 in closing costs. Almost anybody can get a credit card, but someone else determines how much credit you can afford. If you have an address, you can get a welfare check. If you are homeless, don't even think about it. What you used to have doesn't count. It's about what you have now, and if you have nothing in terms of dollars and cents, you get no respect in this country.

Being on welfare does not mean you fare well. The system is designed to perpetuate your failure. People look down on you when you are broke. They act like they are doing you a favor just by taking time to talk to you. It is already humiliating to stand in a welfare line and admit that you cannot provide for your family. Yet, some of the social workers are insulting, abrasive and abusive. They don't realize that without poor people these self-appointed majesties would have no throne. They loud talk you in front of all the people in the lobby. They make you come in at eight o'clock in the morning (you must take your children with you), and they keep you there until four in the afternoon. Once they give you a check, you have to prove every month that you still deserve it. You fill out a form showing that you have not earned any money, you have not given away a car or a boat, no one has moved into or out of your house, and no one gave you more than an hundred dollars. If you don't sign that form by the eleventh of the next month, they stop your check and you have to go down there to reinstate it. Sometimes, even when you do send in the form, they don't get it. No matter. You still don't get your check or your food stamps. Then you have to beg folks who are convinced that it is somehow your fault. If you work, they cut your check. If you get off completely and find a job that pays minimum wages, you forfeit medical benefits. You couldn't pay to continue your medical coverage even if you could afford it because the medical plans only deal with "companies."

I was lucky. My first social worker noticed that I was not the "typical welfare recipient." I was smarter than the average bear. She told me, "You can go to college if you want to. I can help make it work for you. You can get a Pell Grant. It won't affect your check, but it will affect your food stamps." She was my worker for only a few short weeks. Those who came after her seemed to resent the fact that I was in school. When a woman goes into the welfare office seeking help, she does not need a lecture; she needs money. I think every social worker should ask a potential client, "What do you want to be when you grow up?" and then show her how it can be done. She's going to be on welfare anyway. The best thing to do is give her hope for a brighter future, not create ways and means to keep her in the bowels of society.

If you put a welfare mother on the job market before she is ready, she's at the mercy of whoever owns the business. The job could fall through for any number of reasons and, without any specific training, she's back in the system again. Many county offices will be glad to pay for childcare during her first three weeks of employment, but the bad news is that once she starts work, she can't quit without forfeiting her check. If she keeps the job longer than three weeks, she has to pay for childcare. That's $75 a week per child. Most of these women have two or three kids, so childcare could cost as much as two hundred a week. That's almost her whole paycheck, but since $250 a week is more than what she'd get on welfare, it looks pretty good on paper. In terms of dollars and cents, it looks like she's doing okay, but the real deal is that she gets deeper and deeper in the hole and sees no way out. So, she ends up leaving her kids home alone to save the childcare money. Then, if something happens to one of those children, Social Services steps in and takes all of them claiming that she is an unfit mother. They pay $800 a month per child to have them fostered. Can you help me figure out how that makes any sense?

My solution? First of all, the governmental agencies that are dedicated to *welfare reform* need to place some former welfare recipients on their committees. If you take a woman off welfare before she is ready, you set her up for defeat. But if you send that same woman to school for four or five years, she'll have an education that will last for the rest of her life. Think about that for a minute. The "system" uses doctors, lawyers, teachers, nurses, computer specialists, social workers and a whole range of professionals who interact with welfare families and each other. Not everybody on welfare is stupid. A woman who can feed her family on less than $600 a month qualifies as a world class economist. If we train poor people to fill these positions we could re-cycle the benefits of welfare.

But no. We would never do that. We need poverty so that we can measure our own success. We need that evil so we can measure our own goodness. We need defeat and class distinctions so that we can sit back and say, "Look at what's happening to those people."

I did not want to get locked into that system, but when I made up my mind to drop out of college, I knew I was in for the long haul. My older daughter had her baby and moved back to North Carolina. That brought the household income down to $485 a month. Rent was $385. With John's help I was able to survive. I only called him when I absolutely had to, but I became increasingly dependent on him. He never once said "no" to me.

twenty-five

In her book, *Beloved,* Toni Morrison uses a word that most folks think she created: *rememory.* It is actually a word that I've heard women like Aunt Doretta use hundreds of times when they were trying to talk properly. Of course it means all kinds of things to all kinds of people, but it is a way of giving action to a noun, making a verb out of it like *picture* or *jazz.* *Rememory* requires action; you have to go back into your memory and unlock it, remember it, recognize it and allow it to resonate. What I am trying to say here is that I have not forgotten the people who helped me get to this point in my history. Nobody ever does anything alone. Some think they do. Some folks reach every horizon and go beyond it. Then they stand back and say, "Look what I did!' when the truth of the matter is they have had an abundance of help along the way. They forget; but I want you to know that I remember them all. Even though I will not mention all their names, I remember them. They know who they are, and they are not the kind of people who would say, "Humph! She didn't say anything about me."

I tell you this because if there is one thing that pisses me off it is for someone to succeed in a venture and then forget the folks who helped. Okay, make that two things. It really curdles my milk when someone goes through struggle after struggle and finally makes it and then turns her nose up and refuses to help someone else. It should be circular. It should be unconditional. It should not be for self-aggrandizement. There are those, for example, who will help but for the wrong reasons. If the *help-recipient* falters in some way, the helper will say, "After all I've done for you!"

There were good people in my life who saw something that was worth saving. As I have said, I kept the Creative Writing class, and it was in that class that I met two people who would become my Los Angeles "family." They were Steve Cave and Lydia Burke. Without them I never would have made it this far. I felt isolated from the rest of the world and Steve and Lydia were people with whom I could share my story and expect them to understand. They had their own cloudy experiences, so they were not judgmental. They became my dime-store psychologists, you might say. Most of the time I did not need advice; I simply need a listening ear. I needed to say something out loud. I am a firm believer that if you have a problem that you can psychoanalyze yourself, you really shouldn't have a problem. I knew what my problem was: I had a hatred for Hubbie that would not quit. I blamed him for breathing and I carried the hatred into my freedom to the point that I was imprisoned by it. I wasn't free at all. I needed someone to hear my side and be on my side without judgment or condemnation. Steve and Lydia had lived long enough to meet that criteria. They were not picture-perfect or self-righteous. In my writing and in our conversations, they'd both observe my pain and they would share their own "mistakes" so that I wouldn't feel like the only sinful soul.

Steve was from New York. He was good looking, like Langston Hughes. He smoked a pipe, had a snow white widow's peak, was a recovering alcoholic and he was trying to forget his past by making a joke of it. Occasionally, he would make a comment like "dirty dawg" when I spoke of Hubbie, but most of the time he simply assured me that Hubbie was a chapter in my life that did not need rewriting. He said something else, too. He told me that Marva Collins once said, "If you can't make a mistake, you can't make anything."

Lydia was from Bakersfield, and she was writing a book about her life, too. The stories she could tell! I didn't like her at first and I think it was because I was jealous of her. She always smelled of Opium—the real stuff by Yves St. Laurent, not those counterfeits that I used to wear. She was dripping with Gucci and Cartier jewelry and she had an eel skin purse and a leather book bag. She drove a red Datsun 280z, and she didn't work. She didn't have to work; her husband played keyboard for Smokey Robinson.

Lydia was Filipino, not even five feet tall. I was five eight, but every time I stood next to her I felt small. She and her husband had no children, but they were the kind of folks who paid $3000 for a dog they had shipped from England. The dog was a Rottweiler and he only understood German. He was so big that Lydia could ride him.

We were not a perfect match when it comes to friendship. She couldn't give advice about raising kids; she didn't even particularly like children. I couldn't understand her need for the constant companionship of her other dog—a little bitty ball with long hair, of a breed I never learned how to spell and just can pronounce, sounded something like *shit soup*. They lived high on a hill in Studio City; I lived near Temple and Alvarado, the Black and Mexican ghetto. But we had a common bond in that we were both women of color, and we soon discovered that the parallels in our lives by far outweighed the differences.

We became good friends. She thought I was wise, courageous and smart. I thought she was compassionate, forgiving and generous. She "hired" me to do little chores for her. I read her first drafts and proofread her assignments. She paid well to make sure I did not run out of money. When she introduced me to her husband, Sonny, I expected him to treat me like a stray kitten, but he was just as kind as she was. They kept me included at fancy parties, introduced me to Smokey and they gave me respect for what I was trying to do.

Sonny was on tour a great deal and, while he was away, Lydia and I would go shopping, go to the race track or go to the movies. We talked about everything, especially our childhoods, and half the time we acted like two little girls romping through a field of flowers while our hands were sticky with Mary Jane candy. It was a good time for me. I felt connected again.

Lydia saw me through the next few years. She was there for me at the birth of my last child. She supported my decision to keep her. She was there for me when my son was sick, when my second oldest ran away at seventeen to marry some crazy boy, when the rent was due and I didn't have a dime. Lydia was there for me. It was Lydia who introduced me to my second husband, a mistake that's not worth much of my time or yours. Suffice it to say that I was forty-one; he was twenty-five. I was American; he was Egyptian. I was Christian raised; he was Muslim. I was ignorant; he was university educated. I had four kids; he was a virgin. Can you conjure up that image? That's when I decided that whatever it was I was looking for would not be found in a man. The only difference was that when the marriage ended, he was the one who had to leave because it was *my* house.

Lydia helped me get through the shock of John's death simply by acting as a sounding board. I knew he was sick. He had some flu-like symptoms, but I never thought he would die. I had moved to South Central L.A. in April of 1985. John came over to bless the house and he said the weirdest thing: "Looks like you don't need me anymore." He stopped me from visiting him after that; he said he was afraid I'd catch his flu. Then one day in early June he called and asked to see me. When I got there I was shocked at what I saw. John was a very large man, six two and well over three hundred pounds. In his health he looked like Santa Claus. But he'd lost so much weight I hardly recognized him. He was down to one hundred forty pounds. His hair was thin and completely gray. His voice was weak and old. I had the nerve to tell him he looked good. He said, "I know you're lying, but I love you for it. I don't know why…but I just can't seem to shake this thing."

I didn't realize that I would never see him again after that day. I said something stupid like, "Just hang in there and do what the doctor tells you. You'll be fine."

Three months later John was dead. It seemed like he just up and died for meanness, never did tell me he was going. In all the time I had known him, whenever he went to Chicago, or Paris, or Peking, he'd let me know that he was leaving. But he knew he was going to die; he made a special trip home to Stockton to do it, and I was furious with him for not letting me know. He had taught me how to pray away my hatred for Hubbie, and I had prayed hard. I freed up a lot of energy when I stopped hating Hubbie. I moved into my house on Exposition Boulevard under Section 8, and I only had to pay seventy dollars a month rent. I had $167 a month in food stamps and a house full of paid for furniture. Okay, so I didn't need him anymore, but I still wanted him to be near. It seemed that as soon as he recognized that I was *on my feet,* as we say, he died. I was absolutely furious, and Lydia understood my anger.

Steve helped a lot, too. He used to ride his bike to my place. He'd bring a chicken for me to cook and we all ate. He'd spend hours reading what I wrote, offering advice, listening to my defense. He was very patient that way. I'd ask his opinion and then criticize him for giving it. Writers are as protective as mother grizzlies.

But one day Steve came over and he looked a little strange. I couldn't really define the look. At first I thought somebody had died; he looked a little depressed. I was making hamburger patties and, though I did not stop my work, I asked him, "What's the matter with you?"

"It ain't what's the matter with me, Babe; it's what's the matter with you?"

"What are you talking about?"

"Talking 'bout you. What are you doing?"

I looked at my hands, greasy with meat. "I'm making hamburgers for Christ's sake."

"Ah ha."

I'd been in situations like this before. Something was wrong. That was evident. Somebody had done something to him and I was convenient enough for him to purge. "What is that supposed to mean?"

"It means that I just came by here to tell you that I won't be coming anymore."

"Why?"

"Because I am ashamed of you."

"Ashamed of me? What did I do?"

"Nothing."

It looked like we were playing some kind of guessing game and I was too busy to pick up on the clues. "So, if I didn't do anything, why would you stop coming to see us?"

"Well, that's the point. You ain't doing nothing. I thought you said you were going back to school when the baby turned four years old."

"Yes, but—"

"No buts. Kid's been in kindergarten for a few months now. You still ain't doing what you came here to do."

"You just don't understand."

"I understand. I over stand. You're a good writer. I can't stand to see you wasting away like this, so I am not going to be party to it."

That made me mad as hell. I threw raw hamburger at him. "I'm in this house day in and day out taking care of my kids! I don't bother anybody. Now you want to come over here and worry the hell out of me. When you go to the Laundromat you've got one pair of drawers to wash. When you eat a bologna sandwich, everybody in your family has had a meal. You have no idea what it's like. Get the fuck out of my house!"

He left without another word.

There was a small restaurant on the corner and the guy who ran it was tall, sixty-ish, father-like. Everybody, including me, called him Papa. He called me Mama because I fed all the kids in the neighborhood. He had a quiet manner about him and he was good for calming the nerves. After Steve left, I went running to Papa's shop. I told him what had happened. He said, "Well, Mama, you are exactly where you are supposed to be at any given moment. When it's time, you'll make the change."

That did not satisfy me. Steve was right. I wasn't doing anything. Time had dissipated and left me in survival mode. I wasn't doing *anything* that I had planned to do. I went back home and there was a song on the stereo. It was Patti Labelle, *There's a Winner in You*. I listened to the words of that song over and over, and it seemed like it was written just for me:

> It's only me
> I've come to see you
> And I know
> What you've been through
> I will be your friend
> Lean on me for now
> Got to pull you back up

142

Somehow.
And I'll have no more
Of this moping around
I'm tired of you
Putting yourself down
'Cause in spite of all
You've been through
I still believe
There's a winner in you.

The song said the same thing that Steve had said; it just said it in a different way. He had talked to me harshly. Still, I called him and apologized. The next day I went to Los Angeles City College and enrolled in full-time courses. The only problem was, by that time I was terrified at the prospect. I was nearly forty-three years old, had been out of high-school for twenty-six years, and I could not see how I could compete with all those eighteen year old kids whose mothers had a hot meal and clean underwear waiting for them.

I was still grieving John's death. Dealing with that anger and trying to become a college student was very difficult. I wanted to fit in, to *look* like a college kid, so I went to K-Mart and bought a bunch of sweat suits that I could mix and match. I didn't want folks to think that I had bought new clothes for school, so I wore everything once, washed it and hung it on the line to dry. I left the clothes outside all night, and when I went out there the next morning, they were all gone, even my drawers. I was hot! I went running through the house to call the police and I kicked my foot on a piece of furniture. I heard the crack long before I felt the pain. My little toe sat on top of the one next to it. I screamed and fell to the floor.

It hurt so bad I didn't even want to look at it, let alone touch it. I went to the hospital and I guess you know there is not a whole lot they can do for a broken toe...except pull it. The doctor pulled that toe...and I cried all I wanted to. I cried for everything everybody had ever done to me in my life. I cried for everything I had ever done to anybody. I cried until the snot came down and glued my mouth together. I cried for crying. But one thing about it: when I finished crying I felt better. Clean. Purged, you might say. I felt like I had lost weight.

People frequently talk about the strong Black woman. We are the only group on the planet that is not allowed to be weak. Most folks perceive tears as a sign of weakness and, I'll admit, I completely subscribed to that notion.

I see now that I had internalized trouble and powerlessness long enough to do serious damage. But let me tell you this: there is nothing wrong with crying. Tears are water, and water strengthens and nurtures. Without water, nothing and no one can grow. Sometimes you're so busy trying to survive, your eyes get dirty. Crying cleans them and helps you see the world more clearly. It helps you to focus. It gives you new energy. When you finish crying, you can get up and take off. Get a running start and spread your wings. Water is heavy; if you hold onto it, trying to be *strong*, it will weigh you down. But if you shed those tears you can soar.

twenty-six

So there I was on my way to college with an orthopedic shoe, raggedy drawers and a very serious nervous condition. I chose L.A. City because back in '83 I had been impressed with the pedagogy of my English teacher, Mr. G. Jay Kelly. Steve introduced me to him, and Kelly had opened Shakespeare for me and gave me a clear understanding of the classics. He wasn't like Miss Hunt who was my drama teacher in eighth grade. In those days I didn't know anything about looking up the history that informed a play; I was only twelve years old. All I knew was that I didn't understand *Macbeth*, and I asked Miss Hunt to explain it so I could read my part better. She told me, "Don't worry about trying to understand Shakespeare. It's like learning a foreign language. Just do what I tell you." I had let that stand between William Shakespeare and me for all those years. Miss Hunt was one of those *I-got-mine-you-got-yours-to-get* kind of people.

But Kelly wasn't like that. He *loved* Shakespeare, and he wanted us to love him, too. Though he had been teaching at City for almost twenty years, he'd laugh at Falstaff as if it were the first time he'd read the work. I mean he'd throw back his head and belly laugh so hard he'd have to wipe the moisture from his blue Irish eyes. His laughter was contagious. He performed in that classroom. Since I was the kind of student who needed to be entertained, I stayed close to him in an attempt to absorb some of his energy. It was easy to tell that he absolutely adored his work.

So I went back to City College because Jay Kelly taught there.

That year he was teaching Honors English 101. I had to write an essay to get into the class. The question was something about Machiavelli: "It is better to be feared than loved." I didn't know the first thing about writing an essay, but I knew I had to get in that class. I rambled on about how I disciplined my children, put the fear of God and me in their hearts, that kind of thing. There were only twenty spots for the course, and by the time classes started, the essay readers had assigned nineteen of them. Ten of us waited in the hallway. Kelly said that he would read over the ten remaining essays and choose one of us to fill the class.

I panicked. I could not let him deny me entrance into that course. I made a complete pest of myself. I went to his office right after class and told him my name. He said, "Come back at one o'clock." I was back at 12:55. He said, "Come back at three." At three o'clock he still had not had a chance to read the papers, so he said, "Can you come back about nine-thirty Wednesday morning?" I was there at 9:15, and by that time I could recite Shakespeare: *Let me not to the marriage of true minds admit impediments....* He liked that.

"You do understand, don't you, that this is an honors course?"

"Yes," I said.

"And that the workload is intense?"

"Yes, I do."

"When you write an essay, you need to address an issue, argue a point, analyze a character or situation. I don't want to read about cousins, uncles, grandmothers and children."

"Okay." I must have looked pretty silly to him right then. I had a lot of nervous energy, and I was as fidgety as a kid with a red lollipop. "I can do it," I told him. "I know I can do the work."

"Well...since you are so persistent...I have no choice...but to let you in the class."

I thanked him profusely and ran off to take my seat in the classroom before he could change his mind.

My first semester was not bad at all. I learned that Shakespeare was not difficult to read. Some of the language was very similar to the way Grandma Josephine used to speak. A word like *holp,* for example, is something Grandma used to say all the time. It is the past tense of "help." When we read about a "fice" dog, I was the only one in class who knew that Shakespeare was talking about a Chihuahua.

My oldest daughter had moved back home and was out of work, so she kept the house in order. The most difficult time I had during this period was in my Political Science class. The teacher was Dr. Don Wilson, a graduate of UCLA who graded on a curve and insisted that we each write a fifteen-page term paper. He told us to go the library and browse *The Readers' Guide to Periodicals and Literature.* He said it was the only way we could get an 'A' in his class.

The problem was, I could not go to the library. I had not been to a library since I was nine years old. Scared. A childhood trauma, you might say. Whenever I wanted to read a book, I'd just go buy it. But Dr. Wilson insisted on the library and I had to overcome that fear.

This is what happened: When I was little, there was a girl in our neighborhood who used to beat me up all the time. Her name was Helen Jones. She had suffered with TB, and when she went to the Sanitarium, the medicine they gave her made her fat. I was scared of all fat people, but mostly I was scared of Helen. She used to punch me in my stomach and make me cry. She'd hit me in the face and give me a bloody nose. I'd run home to Mama, near collapse, every time.

One day, Mama got tired of it, and she told me, "Next time that girl gets after you I want you to pick up a stick and bust her head."

"But I'm scared of Helen Jones, Mama."

"Scared? Humph! I tell you what…if you don't hit her, I'ma hit you. Now. You want to be scared of Helen Jones *and* me? You better turn her tail upside down and let the rain pour in it."

I surely didn't want a whipping from Mama. She used a peach tree switch and, since it was the spring of the year, the tender young wood would not break; it just wrapped around my legs and left huge whelps everywhere it hit. I'm trying to tell you that if you have never been whipped with a peach tree switch, you ain't been whipped. We moved around a lot in those days, and it seemed like the only requirement Mama had for a new house was that it came equipped with a peach tree in the backyard. So I learned to try to do what she told me. And the very next time Helen Jones tried to beat me up, I picked up a stick and busted her head. I sent her bleeding and running home to her own Mama.

We became friends after that, or, at least I thought we did. I had to pass her house to go just about anywhere, and she'd come running to the front porch just to wave or say, "Hey Barbr'ann." Doesn't that sound like a friend to you?

Anyway, one day I went to the library and got an armload of books. I loved reading about everything. I had a book about wild horses, a book about geography, a couple of song books, etc. As I approached Helen's house I noticed she was playing in the yard. I stopped, just to say, "Hey," and she asked to borrow one of the books. I figured I couldn't read them all at one time, so I let her have one.

About three hours later, Mama came home from work. Without saying a word, she went to the backyard, broke a switch and proceeded to punish me. She whipped me until my legs looked like a scrub board. I didn't know what I had done wrong, so I couldn't promise that I would not do it again. That usually stops a whipping. When she finished, she mocked Helen Jones: "Look, Miss Beulah. Look what Barbr'ann gave me." Then she told me, "Now you go to Helen's house and get that book. Take them *all* back to the library!"

I think Mama's intended message that day was that I should not lend to someone else something that I had borrowed myself. That message was very clear. But she also taught me a fear of the library, and I did not enter one again until Don Wilson made me go.

I'll never forget how I felt when I stood at the foot of that edifice. It looked like the stairs grew a hundred feet tall. I was a grown ass woman, but I was scared to my teeth. My head ached; my palms were cold and wet, and my heart was pumping Kool-Aid. I took one step and got so dizzy that I sank to my knees. I actually crawled up those steps.

By the time I reached the librarian's desk I was out of breath and out of control. I opened my mouth to speak, but no sound came out. I was so weak, I thought I would faint. So I clutched the desk and wrote her a note asking for the "Readers' Guide." She pointed, led me to a table and brought the book to me.

It was a major, major breakthrough. After I recovered I discovered a whole new world, a world that had passed me by for too many years. I started going to the library every day. I looked up stuff that wasn't even assigned to me. I searched every single shelf looking for Black women writers, Black women aviators, Black businesswomen. I wrote a paper in Wilson's class on race discrimination during the Civil War. I wrote a paper in Kelly's class comparing the lives of Henry David Thoreau and Ralph Waldo Emerson. When the semester was over I had 'A's in English, Political Science, Speech and Personal Development. I had a 'B' in Psychology. That gave me a 3.7 GPA. Understand that I am not bragging here. I just want to let you know that after the kind of life I'd led, after the way I had been beaten in my head and face, yes…it did surprise me that I had any sense left.

I took a summer course with Kelly and I earned an 'A' for that, too. In fact, before I finished at City I had eight courses with Jay Kelly. I was addicted to learning. I really liked his style.

In the fall of '88, Don Wilson nominated me to the Student Senate to represent the History Department. I immediately got on several committees and, when I went back to Dr. Wilson to report my progress he said, "I didn't mean for you to get *that* involved."

"Oh?" I said. "Well what exactly did you mean…for me?"

"Well…heh,heh. Well I guess there's no stopping you now, is there?"

"No."

At the time, I meant it with all my heart. Finally, I was doing exactly what I wanted to do, and I loved it. Papa had arranged for me to buy a Volkswagen Rabbit, and I was doing it all. I had proven to myself that I was a survivor, a winner. All the little things that got in the way never even fazed me. I'm talking about things like buying a month's worth of groceries and taking them home on the bus, pretty much the same way we hauled those trunks. I'm talking about wearing shoes with a broken strap and trying to pretend that it had just happened. I'm talking about making the decision to buy a book instead of panties that actually had elastic in them. Survival. Day to day living. Making it happen. That's what I'm talking about.

But there was something going on that was a potential threat, and I thank God now that I did not keep my mouth shut about it. Too many of us suffer in silence, and the fact is, nobody can help you if he or she does not know you are in trouble. My second oldest daughter never did marry that crazy boy, thank goodness. Instead, she graduated from high school, worked for a year and then started college at North Carolina Central University. The oldest girl was in business school in L.A. and was gone all day. My son got out of school at 2:30 in the afternoon, but my grandson and my youngest daughter were in Kindergarten and they finished at 11:30 in the morning.

I had two classes back-to-back with Kelly; one was at 11 a.m. and the other was at 12 noon. I asked a couple of my neighbors to pick up the kids from Kindergarten and keep them until I got home at 1:30. We set up a kind of neighborhood watch/check and balance system. Peaches worked at night, so she *could* go get them. Lula didn't work at all, so if Peaches overslept, Lula could do it. We all looked out for each other's kids. Hell, their kids ate at my house more often than they did at home.

The plan worked for about a week. Then one day I came home late after an emergency meeting of the Student Senate. It was 2:30 in the afternoon and I went to Peaches' house first. She was asleep and had not seen the children. I went to Lula's house and she said, "I think Peaches picked them up." I just about went crazy. I searched the entire neighborhood, knocked on every door. Nobody had seen those children. Finally, I went to the school. By this time it was well past four o'clock. The kids were huddled together in a chair in the office. I knew they were scared, hugging like that, because they didn't even like each other. I broke down and cried. Before I left there, all the secretaries and the principal were crying, too. It was like one of those Oprah reunions.

I talked with Kelly and explained that I did not have a reliable babysitter. He agreed to let me bring the kids to class with me if they could be quiet. I bought each of them a coloring book and a set of crayons. I talked with the school and told them I would be fifteen minutes late every day. I asked them to please keep the kids in the office until I arrived. They agreed to do that.

So for the rest of the semester I would go to my eleven o'clock class, stay there until eleven thirty, get in my Rabbit, take the Hollywood to the Harbor, pick up the kids, and get back to school in time for the last half of my 12 o'clock class.

Like I said, I was doing it all, but it did not come without sacrifice. I was very proud of my daughter at North Carolina Central, and I was committed to doing all I could to help her. I made her clothes, sent her boxes of food and advised her on which classes to take at Central. I thought it was cute; she and I were in college the same time. We were both sophomores, and if I decided to get a four-year degree, she and I would graduate together.

She called in early October 1988 and said something that ultimately sealed my fate: "I need two hundred and fifty dollars." I had the money, but I needed it to pay the gas and electric bills, which meant that I really didn't have the money. "I'll pay it back in December," she said, "After I get my Pell Grant."

I didn't ask her why she needed so much money. She had been on her own since she was seventeen years old. She had finished high school and worked two jobs to buy herself a car. She saved her money and put herself through the first year of her schooling, and she never asked me for a quarter. How could I not help her now? I want you to know that this was not one of those things that just happened and I had to learn to live with it. No, this was a conscious choice. I sent my baby that money.

In less than a week the Department of Water and Power turned off my electricity. Two days later, the gas company followed suit. I believed I was doing the right thing. Damn it all, I knew I was doing the right thing. I came to the decision, however, that maybe it wasn't the right time to do the right thing. I should wait until she finished at Central and my other daughter finished Business College. I should wait until I finish raising my children. I was asking them to sacrifice way too much. My son was too young to understand why he couldn't have a Nintendo. The baby girl was too smart to be denied a set of encyclopedia. My grandson was too adventurous to be ignored.

It was a conscious choice.

I went to see Jay Kelly, and I'll admit I was full of water. I felt the need to escape. I tried to no avail to keep the conversation light.

"It looks like I'll have to put my dreams on hold one more time. But I want you to know that you have made a great impact on my life." I forced a smile. "I want to be just like you when I grow up."

He said, "You're such an asset to the class. I'd hate to lose you."

That just about broke my heart, and the stupid, stubborn, selfish tears welled up and spilled over and I could have kicked myself for crying in front of him.

"Thanks."

"Listen. You have until December 14th to drop. Why don't you wait? Take a few days off to think. Maybe things will get better."

"Maybe I can get a job at the Post Office or something. I feel like I am asking too much of my children. They need me to be their mother."

"You can do that and this, too." He took a long, deep breath and puffed out his jaws as he exhaled. "You know, people look at me and think I don't have a care in the world. But I've had hard times. I've had to eliminate people from my life because they simply weren't going in the same direction. You can make it through this. Just remember the words of Nietzsche: *That which does not kill me makes me stronger.*"

That which does not kill me makes me stronger. I thought about that long and hard. I looked over my life and realized that with all that had happened, with every difficult encounter, every obstacle, I had emerged stronger, more competent and more determined to make it. I could get through this and stay in school. I could.

At home that evening I lit a candle and studied by candlelight. For three weeks I cooked every meal, even grits, on an hibachi. We bathed in cold water, or showered at Lula's house. When the car broke down, I walked the seven miles to City College. I washed clothes on a scrub board in the bathtub. I read books to my children, told stories, made up games, sang songs. Jay Kelly was my hero; he saved my life. And I was not running away anymore.

PART III
FREEDOM

twenty-seven

In the spring of 1989 I ran for and was elected as President of the Student Senate. The term was for the 89-90 school year, and that election made me an Administrative Vice-President of the Associated Students' Organization. I planned a Thanksgiving dinner for impoverished students and the homeless people in the college community, and I started collecting food during the summer. I didn't do it because I wanted gratitude or glory. I did it because I had to. I had been homeless; I was still poor. While I had made Hurston's words my motto, and was determined to "wrassle me up a future or die trying," I now believed that I was unconquerable, and that belief alone was enough to make me want to save and celebrate the world.

I knew, too, that nothing had to be the way it was for me. All I had to do was step outside my door and look at the empty, hopeless faces that walked my street. I guess I wanted to show that I knew how to recognize and receive a blessing. I knew how to be thankful. I knew how to acknowledge a debt to God, even though I believed then as I do now, that one can never repay such a debt. There is an old spiritual song that says, "You can't beat God giving, no matter how you try. The more you give, the more He gives to you." I am a witness to that truth.

The Thanksgiving dinner was the first time I noticed the truth of that song. Members of the Senate and I collected enough food to feed over six hundred people. We got five hundred dollars from ASO, but the rest came from the community, the faculty, students and clubs on campus. Senate members did all the cooking. Faculty helped to serve and clean up. Even the president of the college rolled up his sleeves, put on an apron and went to work. It was a marvelous feast of turkey and ham, potatoes and gravy, vegetables, beans, macaroni and stuffing. Fruits of all kinds, and cakes and pies fit for a king. As the folks left, we gave them care packages that contained Top Ramen, Beanie Weenies, juice, toothpaste and soap. When it looked like we were going to run out of food before we fed everybody, some of the senate members cooked spaghetti. Then we found several cases of Oodles of Noodles that had been donated by the Buddhist Club, and we kept feeding hungry people. It reminded me of the story of Jesus and the Multitude. Every time we thought it was all over we found more food to give away—canned ravioli, corned beef hash—and we didn't close our doors until hours later when there was no one else in line.

That was the day I realized the benefit of my age, and I became acutely aware of the accuracy of Grandma Josephine's prediction. I had taken the children to North Carolina to celebrate Grandma. Her birthday was May 13, but since that was so close to Mother's Day, we always honored her during Memorial Day weekend. That particular year, 1987, Grandma was a hundred years old. My kids and my grandson were excited about meeting her because I had told them that she had brown skin and white hair. My grandson, Doubting Thomas that he was, could not imagine his grandma having a grandma. He said, "Brown skin and white hair? There's no such thing, Grandma!"

When we got to North Carolina it was dark. We'd been on the bus for three days and I had not seen my parents in five years. I wanted to spend time with them so I could catch up on who got married, who split up, who had a baby, who died. Of course I had to listen to them rant and rave about how fat I was, how long I had been gone, why didn't I write more often? So we didn't go see Grandma right away. My grandson was antsy all night; he couldn't even sleep. He said he was sure I had told him a story.

After breakfast the next morning we all walked to Grandma's house. My grandson ran ahead and went into the house first. Just as we entered the yard, he came running out of the house at neck-breaking speed, fell off the porch and bounced up breathless: "Come on! You gotta see this! It's true! She's got brown skin and white hair! I never saw anything like it in my whole life!"

Grandma met us at the front porch and sat down in her rocking chair, smiling. The kids stared at her for a long time. Her skin was very wrinkled, and that was something new to them. Her cloud of hair was parted in the middle and corn-rowed on each side. The braids fell softly on her chest. There were five generations on that porch and it occurred to me that I wanted to know her better. Grandma was an old lady when I was born, and she was never anything but my grandmother. There had to be more to her and I wanted to know what it was. I needed to know my own history. All I knew about her early life was that her mother had died when she was twelve and she had to raise her siblings. I said, Grandma, one day I am going to come here with a pencil and paper, buy you a Pepsi and a bag of peanuts, and I want you to tell me everything you remember."

The Pepsi and peanuts were a part of the ritual of sitting on the porch, watching the sun set and talking about anything. It was a game, of sorts, that Grandma played with us when we were children. We'd open the Pepsi and pour the peanuts inside the bottle. Then we'd savor the flavor of salt and sugar and crunch on a peanut after we swallowed a mouthful of soda. It was a silly game, but a tricky one. The object was to finish the soda and the peanuts at the same time. Most of the time there was one stubborn peanut that stayed stuck at the bottom of the bottle after the drink was gone. So the next step, and this was the tricky part, was to suck that bottle until it released the last peanut. Grandma was the best at that and, I don't know, maybe I was trying to recapture something from days gone by—the good feelings of childhood, or something, but Mrs. Josephine Artis Sherrod said to me: "That's right well. But I don't drink Pepsi no mo'. I switched to Co'Coly 'bout three yeah ago."

I couldn't believe that Grandma would interrupt a history I'd known all my life. I was hurt. I felt hollow, the way I felt when I walked my last child to her first day of school. It was almost as if I had been clinging to something that never existed. For a minute I thought I was going to cry. Then I got downright mad.

"Three years ago? You were ninety-seven years old!"

"Well, Bob Ann…ya never git too ole to change yo min'."

The expanse of a million years had passed since anyone had called me that. Bob Ann, Bobbie Ann, Bob, Barbr'ann were all names that I answered to when I was a child. At least that had not changed. I had begun to feel like a wayward daughter with no roots, but when Grandma called me by that name I felt connected again. Though I was still a little puzzled, I was fairly satisfied, but Grandma had more to say.

"You gon' change, too one day. Ain't gon' be 'bout no Pepsi or Co'Coly. Gon' be sumpin' big. Gon' be sumpin' good. Gon' be 'bout whatcha lef' heah fuh. Ain't gon' be whatcha thank, but hit'll be what God wont. An' He gon' hep ya, if ya hep yo'sef. Look to me like you already done holp yo'sef right much."

Grandma died the following year, about a month before her next birthday. I did not grieve for her; I rejoiced and celebrated her life. Her words had left me completely bewildered until the Thanksgiving dinner. I noticed that I was in charge. Even Dr. Young, the president of the college, asked me for instructions. The students in the senate took their directions from me, and there was no question, no argument, no debate, no discussion and no doubt that I was the boss that day.

155

I looked around that room and realized that we were all as one. Though my colleagues were half my age, most of us were parents. Most of us had to struggle just to struggle. People are always talking about the light at the end of the tunnel; most of us were still looking for the tunnel. There was no organized help for us; we only had each other. That was the day I decided to start my own college. I would establish a college that could grow into a university. It would be geared to meet the needs of the returning student. There would be an elementary school and a nursery right there on campus. Maybe we could even have bi-coastal campuses. I'd make sure that my students would never have to worry about child care. They'd never have to worry about whether to buy groceries or the book they needed. And they would never have to worry about a place to stay.

The first Black feminists had a motto: *Lifting as we climb.* That was my mission in life. I could teach. I could spread the word and guide someone else to her personal freedom. I didn't have a nickel, but I could make some money and save some money. I had won several scholarships because I could "persevere in the face of adversity." Perhaps I could apply for a grant to help other students like me. If Bethune could do it with a dollar and a quarter, I could hustle up some money from somewhere and start that school. Maybe I'll talk with whomever is running the country when the time comes.

But first I had to finish my own education.

In December of that year, while we were on Christmas break, the dean ran a grade check on all the student government officials. Out of seventeen members of ASO, it turned out that I was the only one who was qualified. Some did not have the 'C' average. Some had not paid their dues. Some were not registered in enough courses, and one was not registered at all. Overnight I became the president, executive vice-president, administrative vice-president and treasurer all rolled into one. There were sixteen thousand, nine hundred students at Los Angeles City College. They represented a hundred different countries and they spoke sixty-eight different languages. I was responsible for their welfare.

Of course, the out-going president was irate when he heard the news. He made phone calls to the dean and wrote letters to the local, district and regional administrations. He hired a lawyer to look for "loopholes." He even got the media involved by writing a letter to *Los Angeles Times.* The Student Organization of Latinos (SOL), which he founded, refused to cooperate with me. They were a very powerful group, the largest on campus, and the out-going president and they tried to sabotage every effort I made. But while he was busy making calls and writing letters, while he was busy trying to justify why he had not paid his dues, while he was busy trying to convert to an evening student so that six units would be enough to keep him in office, I was busy taking inventory.

We had a budget of eighty-seven thousand dollars and by December, almost all that money was gone. He had spent four thousand dollars on stationery. I called in every name plate, every staple gun, every note pad. I froze all the accounts and made sure that no one could get so much as a pencil without my signature. I held a special election and made sure that the dean checked each individual's qualifications before he approved their candidacy. It was a tempest around there for nearly a month, but when the dust settled, my appointment was official. I was the president of ASO.

I was very fortunate. I had the full support of the Student Senate. The vice-president moved up to the presidency of the senate after I left. His name was Juan and he was also a very influential member of SOL. He explained to them the logistics of what had happened, and he urged them to cooperate with me. Jay Kelly became my advocate. Since he taught five classes with an average of thirty students in each, he was able to solicit support from a large group. One young woman who had heard me speak at the Thanksgiving dinner, came into the office one day and said, "You the new female Jesse Jackson, Honey." Then there was another young woman who came with her own entourage. Her name was Carolyn Rody.

I had worked with Carolyn on many occasions at bake sales, Halloween parties for elementary school children in the community, and especially in Alpha Gamma Sigma. She was president of that society, and she was very popular on our campus. I knew she was smart; she got 'A's in physics and calculus, but I did not have a clue to the scope of her brilliance until I became president of ASO.

"I've been on this campus for eight years," she said. "And I've never seen anything like that Thanksgiving dinner."

"Really?"

"Really. Most people *want* to do something, but they complain that there is not enough money to do it. They want to make it perfect. But you just got busy and put it together with practically no money. I think you are going to be a great president."

"Thank you. It's kinda scary. There is so much that I don't know how to do."

"But you will learn, and you will do it. I think it is fate. You need an advisory council. I won't be your chief, but I'd be happy to serve on it. Here's my number. Call if you need me."

I can't tell you how many times I called that number over the next few weeks. Sometimes I had a question; Carolyn had the answer. Sometimes I just needed an encouraging word; Carolyn had that, too. When I decided to appoint Ralph Frankfort Meredith (I loved to say that name) as my chief advisor, Carolyn supported that decision because he'd had experience with the former president.

Carolyn Rody was tall, slender and shapely. She looked like a Nubian princess. She wore a short-cropped Afro and horn-rimmed glasses. Every day she had on something leather—a tight leather skirt or leather pants or leather bustier. She always had money, and she was eager to treat somebody to lunch. I never saw her alone; there was at least half a dozen folks around her at any given time. She was forceful, opinionated and very well-read. In fact, it was Carolyn who introduced me to Toni Morrison's works and bought *The Bluest Eye* for me.

I finished reading that book at ten o'clock at night, and I called Carolyn immediately. We talked until four in the morning about the book, the characters, the way our lives intersected with theirs. We told each other secrets we had harbored since childhood. Though she was twenty-six and I was almost forty-five, we recognized the parallels in our lives, our upbringing, my mama, her mama and theirs. I found it easy to talk with her, and I eventually told her why I could identify with Pecola in *The Bluest Eye*.

During my first semester at City I had taken a course in speech that required us to keep a journal. The name of the textbook was *Looking Out, Looking In: Communicating with Myself*. I had to answer questions in the book by writing in my journal. Some of them seemed pretty silly to me: *What is your favorite color? Why? What is the first thing in your house that you want people to see? Why? Are you a sexual being? How do you define intimacy?* But some of them were not so silly. *How do you respond to anger? How do you react to death? How do you feel about touching?*

That last one got me every time. I was very thorough in my journal; the teacher said so, but I kept avoiding that question each time it appeared and it came up in every chapter. I just didn't want to confront that issue because I was afraid that if I went that far inside I'd fall in and never come out. That's what happened to Pecola. She went deep inside herself and stayed there. Crazy. Pitiful. And it is a miracle that it didn't happen to me. Then, too, our situations were quite different. For one thing, I never thought I was ugly, never wanted blue eyes. For another, he wasn't my father; he was a cousin. And, finally, my Mama didn't beat me when she found out. In fact, she did absolutely nothing as I told you earlier.

I think that's where my ideas about sex got all screwed up. For many years I thought that my mother blamed me for what happened. He was still her favorite nephew but I was a nasty girl. At least, that's the way I took her reaction. So, for a long time I was not able to relax and enjoy myself with a man. I felt guilty whenever I felt good because I thought of it as nasty. Thinking nasty intensified the pleasure, and the pleasure intensified the guilt.

Now I know that women have always had to deal with our bodies being accessible to any male. Cousins, brothers, uncles, fathers and neighbors alike seem to think they can violate us with impunity. I can't tell you how many books I have read on that subject, but I can tell you that if I had not read *The Bluest Eye,* neither Carolyn nor you would have ever heard it from me.

That's when I learned that literature has a greater purpose than mere entertainment. Some books can bring us face-to-face with our own realities. I reached inside *The Bluest Eye* and pulled out a piece of myself. I went back into *I Know Why the Caged Bird Sings* and found another piece. I found even more in *The Color Purple* and recently, when I read *The Help,* I discovered even more of me.

Bit by bit I was getting stronger, more complete. We have to reconcile with our past in order to become whole. Pauline beat the shit out of Pecola, drove her crazy and made her baby die. Angelou's uncles killed the man who touched her, and that silenced her for years. Minnie's husband beat her and, like my mother, she was the financial strength in her family.

Carolyn paid attention to my story and the way I identified with the things I read. She was the best listener I've ever known. Like you, she did not interrupt; she just listened to me purge myself of the guilt I had harbored for years. Over the next few months she would feel my pain, share my joy, defend my decisions and support me in times of crisis.

During the spring of 1990 I was asked to host the Dean's Honor Tea. Carolyn and her husband Matthew bought me a new wardrobe and I was eager to display my fashion-conscious self. We had an allocation of ten thousand dollars for the tea, but since we had been so successful with the Thanksgiving dinner, I decided to transfer most of that money somewhere else. I paid my oldest daughter fifty dollars to prepare the Swedish meatballs, and I got volunteer students from ASO to do the rest. One of them complained to me: "I swear, we have been some cooking mother fuckers since you took office. Every time we hit this campus, we got a bag."

But the tea went off without a hitch. There was plenty food; everybody was happy, and I started to look at what Carolyn had said about "fate." It was fate that brought me to L.A. Fate brought me to City College. Fate let me enter college at just the right time to catch Jay Kelly in English 101. Fate led me to apply for transfer to USC. Fate allowed me to announce my acceptance on the night of the tea. Every course I took with Kelly filled some requirement at USC; that was fate at work, too. It was fate that let me meet Carolyn Rody. We were destined to be good friends.

twenty-eight

University of Southern California was a part of my dream. It was only four blocks away from my house and I wanted to go there so badly. The kids and I would walk through the campus at least once a week on our way to the village or when we went to the Coliseum. I loved the aura of the school, the smell of it, the promise it offered. Because I was broke, however, I thought UCLA was my destiny, but that would require a two hour bus ride one way. Four hours on the bus each day made no sense. I needed to be closer in case my children had an emergency.

South Central L.A. was dangerous. My kids learned early how to "hit the dirt" when the bullets flew. We lived on Exposition Blvd., a fairly neutral street, but the Crips were directly behind us and the Bloods were in front. My children went to school in Bloods territory and an occasional gun battle in the vicinity of the school often left innocent people wounded or dead.

I spoke with Ann Cade-Wilson about the possibility of finding money to fund my education at USC. She was the director of the Transfer Center at City. She looked at my records and said, "Oh, Honey. You don't need any money to go to USC. You have a beautiful transcript! They will be happy to pay your way."

She was right. USC gave me a full scholarship. Here again, fate stepped in and took control. USC sits in the middle of the Black and Hispanic communities, yet its student population was predominantly white. The year I was accepted was the inaugural year of the Neighborhood Outreach Program, and the powers that be had determined to diversify student enrollment.

I was so ignorant, I almost dropped out before I even got started. I went to orientation. I even went to all my classes on the first two days, but when I counted all the books I had to buy, I was looking at about five hundred dollars that I did not have. I was sick in the pit of my stomach, and I headed home with a heavy heart. On my way I noticed a long line of people at the Financial Aid office. I got in line, too. I figured that I could go in there and ask for a loan. That way I could get the books and pay them a little at a time. It wouldn't hurt to ask. The worst thing they could say was "No."

It took more than half an hour for me to reach the window, and when I got there I explained to the man that I needed a loan to buy my books. He said, "We're running behind in our financial aid packages. Give me your social security number and I'll have somebody look up your file. Come back in twenty minutes. Don't stand in line again; just come back to this window."

So I waited the twenty minutes and went back. The man said, "I still don't have your file; we're so busy today. But if you'll wait a few minutes more, I'll do it myself."

I waited again. He seemed like such a nice guy and I didn't know how to take him because I was not accustomed to *nice.*

The man came back to the window a few minutes later and he said, "Ms. Lewis?"

I said, "Yes?"

He said, "You've got a lot of gift aid here."

I said, "And?"

He said, "And the university owes you this much money." He drew a circle around the bottom line. I almost choked on my spit, but I was cool.

I said, "Well could I get part of it, or a loan or something so I can buy my books?" I was thinking that I'd have to wait until December to get the money.

He said, "Oh, just take this over to that window and tell the person there, 'Gimme my money now!'" He smiled then, so I thought he was joking. But nearly everybody else was going to that window, so I decided to give it a try.

There was a young woman there and I said to her: "That man over there told me to come here and demand that you give me my money. But I am too much of a lady to do that, so could you please tell me what to do next?" I handed her the paper. She left the window for a minute, and when she returned, she gave me a check for two thousand, eight hundred and fifty-three dollars.

I received a refund check like that at the beginning of every semester. That money kept me going. It kept my family fed. It bought my son a Sega Genesis and supplied him with baseball cleats and football jerseys. It bought beautiful dresses for the baby girl because she was forever into something at school. It also bought me a word processor so I could do my work more effectively. USC was good to me. The university let me know that it wanted me as badly as I wanted to be there. I had tried to go there before I went to City, but it was far too expensive. Now, I had a free ride and all I had to do was earn good grades. I knew I could do that because I had a 3.83 GPA at City College and I came to realize that if you are an 'A' student at LACC you are an 'A' student anywhere.

I decided to concentrate on my grades and stay away from politics. That was a good move. My son and daughter were at the age where they had their own little things going, and they expected me to be there. That was only fair; I kept them involved in everything I did. They have been to more lectures, concerts, plays, college classrooms, banquets, art exhibits, poetry readings and "brain" parties than any seven and ten year olds should have to endure. It was only fair that I should attend their events.

My son had been playing organized sports since he was five years old. He even played when he was sick, and he was sick a lot. I spent so much time in the emergency room that the doctors and nurses called me by my first name. They kept sending him from one specialist to another and they did all kinds of allergy tests, one of which required forty-two needle pricks in his back. The doctors said they were going to put tubes in his ears and remove his adenoids, but for four years they never did anything except pump him full of antibiotics. As soon as he'd get rid of one infection, damned if he didn't go into another one. He'd cry so pitifully. One day he told me, "Ma, I got headache. It hurt me so bad." And there I was off again to the emergency room.

I told that doctor, "You've been telling me for years that you're going to do something to help him. I can't stand it any longer. It makes me want to beat him up just because he's hurting!"

Oh yeah, they scheduled the operation then. Doctors don't want to hear about you beating up on a kid. They put in the tubes; they removed those offensive adenoids, and after that, whenever my son caught a cold, he got over it like any other child. It used to be that I could hear him breathing from any point in the house. Now, he was so quiet, I'd sneak into his room to make sure he was still alive.

He started playing baseball with a T-ball league. Those little tykes played for all they were worth. I'd take my books to the game and I'd only put them down when my kid was at bat. He'd crack that ball and we'd both take off running. I'll bet I have run a thousand bases during his sports career. One thing about it, I was there at every game. He could always look over his shoulder and see me. Today, he is a high school football coach, and I still go to every one of his games.

Doing everything is the easy part. Doing it well and quickly, that's hard. I signed up for a course in contemporary literature with Professor Carol Muske-Dukes. She had quite a reputation. She was a renowned poet and the author of the novel, *Dear Digby*. I stopped by her office one day in December and I said, "I am a slow reader. I was wondering if you would tell me what will be on the syllabus so I can start reading during the Christmas break.

She seemed to like that, and she wrote a list of books on a piece of paper and handed it to me. She said she could tell that I would be great in her class, and she asked me if I write. When I said "yes," she invited me to take one of her poetry classes.

One thing I learned right away: I may be a whole lot of things, but a poet I am not. It's like Hubbie used to say, *You can't make chicken salad out of chicken shit.* I didn't quite have the vocabulary to write poetry. But I was older than Carol and she gave me respect for my experiences. She became my mentor, my friend. She wrote letters of recommendation for scholarships that I won. When I approached her in my senior year and told her that I wanted to go to graduate school, Carol encouraged me to do it. She wrote a letter in support of my application, and she gave me the money for the Graduate Record Examination.

When I took the GRE there was a little box to check if I were interested in fellowship monies. Of course, I checked that box and the Ford Foundation sent me an application that I immediately filled out and returned. In my statement of purpose I told them about studying by candlelight and washing clothes on a scrub board. In November and December of 1991 I applied to Duke, Cornell and USC. Duke and Cornell rejected me before they cashed my checks for the application fees. I stopped payment on the checks. I was admitted to USC's graduate program in February of 1992. In March I received an offer letter for an All-University Fellowship. It would pay all my tuition and fees and I would get a stipend of fourteen thousand dollars a year. I was beside myself with joy and relief. I could go to grad school. I could live on fourteen thousand. I could get off welfare.

Then one day in early April, I picked up the baby from school. My son was at practice, so she and I had a couple of hours to ourselves. The day before that three things had happened that let me know we needed to spend some quality time together.

First, she was playing outside with her friends when suddenly she came running into the house. "Mom, are you a virgin?" she asked.

"Ah...no," I replied. Before I could determine the impetus behind the question she was out the door. I heard her tell her friends, "See, I told you. My mother is not a virgin and neither am I 'cause I am just like her!"

I called her to come inside. She did, but she was the one in control of the conversation: "Where did I come from?"

That was the second thing. I sat her on my lap and told her everything I knew about the birds and the bees. Child-raising experts tell us that if they

164

are old enough to ask, they are old enough to know. I thought, perhaps some of it would make her uncomfortable, so I asked, "Does that scare you?"

"No. I already knew that. I read your biology book."

"Okay, well, why did you ask?"

"Because I want to know where I came from. My friends say I am adopted because I am dark-skinned and I don't look like anybody else in the family. My sisters came from New Jersey. You and my brother are from North Carolina. Where did I come from? Was I out here in California all by myself?"

I assured her that she was not adopted, and I explained the color genes as best I could.

The third thing that happened that day has kept me on guard ever since. I was busy cooking and cleaning, and it looked like the child followed me everywhere. With every move I made she was right there in my way. At one point I stepped on her foot, and finally, I turned around and asked her, "What are you doing?"

She said, "I am following in your footsteps."

She was my best friend, and that let me know we needed to do some "girl stuff." We stopped to get ice cream and then we walked home giggling and singing that song where you have to skip and change feet every time you say "left" or "right":

I left, left
Left my wife and four little children
Right, right,
Right in the middle of the road...

There was a letter in the mailbox from the Ford Foundation. I held it in my hand for a long time, just looking at it. Then I took my daughter and the letter to my room and I threw it on the bed. I sat down and pulled her to my lap. She said, "What's the matter?"

"Nothing."

"What's that?"

"Letter."

"Open it."

"No."

"Why?"

"Scared."

"I'll open it. I'm not scared of anything."

And she did. The first word she read was "Congratulations!"

I jumped to my feet and dropped my baby on the floor. I had just left

165

campus, but I grabbed her and the letter and went running down to USC. Carol had a late class. When I got there I was out of breath. I found a seat in the back of the room and Carol, seeing me with my child and, apparently, thinking something was wrong, gave her class a fifteen minute break.

"What's the matter?" she said anxiously. I couldn't say a word. I just handed her the letter. She started to read and all of a sudden she said, "Yes! Yes!" and hugged me. None of the class had taken that break, so I had a con-gratulating, handshaking, neck-hugging audience. It was the most exciting moment of my life thus far.

The Ford Foundation paid for tuition and fees, too, but my stipend was only eleven thousand five hundred. The federal government would not al-low me to take both grants, so I went to see the dean. I told her, "I would really like to take the Ford because of the honor and prestige. But honor and prestige do not a bologna sandwich make. I have two kids to feed."

We laughed and talked for an hour that day. She said, "Darling, this is wonderful! It's what we like to see. This way we can help someone else. We can combine your grants so that you will have three years of support for your studies, and we will tack on a dissertation year. How's that?"

I thought that was just grand. There were two heads in that room coming together to make things work, two beautiful Black women on the move, and two women named Barbara. One was Dr. Barbara Solomon, Dean of USC's Graduate School; the other was Barbara Williams Lewis, Ford *and* All-University Fellow.

twenty-nine

I hope you don't mind all the Cheeveresque or Faulknerian detail I give you. I want you to know how things happened for me and how I dealt with them. Maybe they can help you in whatever you're trying to do. If it begins to sound like advice, just remember that advice is something you can take or leave. "Take what you need; throw the rest away." That's my motto. That's my ruling passion. It is really weird how the universe starts to work against you when you get close to fulfilling your dreams. It's like the message in that song, *God Bless the Child:* "You can help yourself, but don't take too much." I've always been the kind of person who would set a goal for myself, and once that goal was accomplished, I'd set another one. Even as a child I had big dreams about what I would do with my life. I used to dream of flying, soaring through the air like Peter Pan and Tinker Bell. I dreamed about dancing. Ah me, I even tried to act on that dream. I used to dance in the yard on Vance Street and I was convinced that one day Pearl Bailey would drive by in her yellow Cadillac, discover me and tell the whole world that I was the greatest ballerina of all time. Sometimes I'd dream about climbing a huge hill. I started out in my daddy's mint green Packard. I was driving, and the hill kept getting higher and higher until it reached the sky and the Packard turned into a bicycle, then a scooter and then roller skates until finally, I was barefoot and at the top of the hill, but there was not room enough for me to stand up because the sky pressed down on my back.

I used to dream that God chose me to save the world and all I had to do was wave my hand and there was no more poverty, no more hunger, no more sickness, no more war, no more backstabbing, no more confusion, no more prejudice, no more sin and no more deflated dreams. Oh, I had some serious dreams. But the universe has a way of letting you know that dreams don't always come true. The universe throws little obstacles at you to test your strength. Things don't just fall out of the sky just because you say you want them. You have to work at it. You have to really want it. I'm not talking about *I'd like to have…* or *Wouldn't it be nice if…?* I mean you have to want it so badly that everything else takes second place. Fix your mind on this: If you can dream, you can develop a plan. With that plan, the dream becomes the truth.

My graduation at USC was set for May 4, 1992. Exactly thirty years had passed since I graduated from high school, but it seemed like the closer I came to fulfilling my dreams, the more the rest of the world fell apart. My oldest daughter drove me to Crenshaw Mall to buy stockings for that special day. As we were leaving the mall I noticed that a crowd of teenagers had gathered in the parking lot. At first I thought they had gotten out of school early that day for senior privileges or something. Then I noticed that they were an angry mob. They opened doors and jumped into moving cars, ignoring the protests of the drivers. When they got to our car, a young man said, "Clear the way. Let these ladies through!" As we escaped the parking lot, one of them said, "This is for Rodney, sisters." It was April 29, 1992.

In the previous year, a Black man named Rodney King had been severely beaten by some white policemen. Four of those cops were on trial for that beating. The verdict had just come in and the cops were acquitted.

There were so many injustices that seemed to be peculiar to South Central. The Black community was still fuming over the death of fifteen year-old LaTasha Harlins.

Harlins was shot and killed by a Korean merchant when the two of them argued over a bottle of orange juice. The judge suspended a five-year sentence for the merchant and gave her five years' probation. Within the month, that same judge sentenced another woman to thirty days in the county jail for leaving her dog locked up in her car while she went shopping. People thought about that and the anger swelled like a yeast roll.

So, when the acquittal of those cops came in, Los Angeles exploded. Folks took to the streets chanting, *No justice; no peace.*

Driving was difficult because of so many people in the street, but my daughter dropped me off at home and then called to say that she had arrived home safely. We called each other every half hour or so and we both turned on our televisions.

The first thing I noticed was the beating of Reginald Denny. I lived at Exposition and Normandy. Florence and Normandy was only about a mile away. The second thing I noticed was that fires began to crop up everywhere. The sky turned dark, like one big black cloud. The whole neighborhood smelled like a smoked ham hock. Folks were torching the businesses and then looting them. People ran through the streets every which way. Traffic was horrendous; all the lights were out. I saw a truckload of kids speeding up and down Exposition shouting, *No justice; no peace!* and waving their fists in the air.

My baby screamed, "Oh God! Why is this happening?" I looked at my child and she had changed colors. She was a dull gray, and her face was swollen with tears. I had to practically snatch her out of the air because she was running and screaming, "We're gonna die! We're gonna die!"

I held her close to me. Her little heart was beating so fast I could see it through her shirt. I said, "Just calm down. Everything is going to be all right."

She said, "No! We're gonna die!"

"No… we are not going to die. Everything will be fine. You'll see."

"But I don't know why this is happening."

"Neither do I. But you know…God went through so much trouble to bring you and me together. He's not going to let anything happen to us now."

That seemed to calm her a bit and she eventually went to sleep. She awoke an hour later and she was screaming again. "Mommy, mommy, mom-meee!" She'd had a bad dream. She said that two white trains were going in different directions on the railroad track in front of our house.

"You were coming from the dairy. One of the trains hit you and knocked you into the other one and all I could do was scream, 'Mommy!' I couldn't do anything to help you."

"You don't have to help me," I told her. "My job is to help you, to protect you and love you up every day."

I took her to the front porch. I wanted her to see the destruction and realize that we had lived through it. There were two white automobiles overturned on the railroad track. One was headed east towards USC; the other was headed west towards Normandy. That's when I noticed the third thing. People of all colors, shapes and sizes ran through the streets with pillow cases full of stuff. Guys drove trucks through the Laundromat, the hamburger joint, the stereo shop. Folks passed by our house with sofas on their backs, televisions under their arms, guns in their hands. I wagered that half of them could not even spell *civil rights*. There were no police in sight.

The next day was worse. I had errands to run, so I locked the kids in the house and left without them. Looters did their thing in broad daylight. Folks plowed their cars into other cars just because they didn't like the looks of the occupants. Los Angeles was in a state of emergency. The National Guard arrived. I had to go to the post office and pick up my check under the watchful eye of armed guards. Then my daughter had to drive me all the way to Alvarado and 7th Street before we could find a check cashing place that was open. What I saw during that trip was like something in a horror movie. The city I loved smoldered in some parts and blazed out of control in others. There were gutted buildings and wrecked cars. None of the traffic lights worked. So many people roamed the streets we could hardly move the car. Korean merchants paced their roofs armed with Uzies, 9MM's and Tech 9's. A Church's Chicken restaurant was boarded up with ply wood and spray painted, "Black Owned."

We parked the car on Bonnie Brae, and when we got back to it, the back window had been broken and the stereo was gone. My four hundred and fifty dollars' worth of books were still on the back seat. Few thieves see value in books, I guess.

We drove up 7th Street and turned left on Normandy, thinking that it was the fastest and safest way home. We had to stop at Olympic, however, because we simply could not get through. That was the first time I saw a policeman; just one was sitting under a tree near the intersection. There were thousands and thousands of Koreans. They came from every direction, and for a minute it looked like they were surrounding our car. My heart quickened. I envisioned us being hanged, mutilated and burned. I said to my daughter, "Get us out of here." And she said, "I don't think they are after us, Mama. Looks like they are going to pray."

She was right. They gathered at the park to pray. I was sure they wanted peace; their businesses had been the hardest hit, but the whole scene had taken all the starch out of me.

USC cancelled finals because of the riots, but I still had a take-home exam that was due that afternoon. I did not want to go back into the war zone, so I called the TA and tried to explain that it was too dangerous for me to make it to campus. She told me that she did not have the authority to cancel or postpone the paper because the professor was in Paris. I said, "Don't you know that South Central is on fire?" And she said, "Yes. But I live in Burbank and am, therefore, unaffected." Then she laughed.

Can you imagine that kind of ignorance? Can you even fathom any-one stupid enough to deny that when a part of America is in trouble *all* of America is in trouble? When one person's civil rights are violated we are all at risk of violation. It goes right back to what I was telling you about the king of dogs. Nobody recognizes persecution unless it happens to him or her per-sonally. Otherwise it's *those* people and the others think they are *unaffected*.

The rioting lasted for the best part of three days. Rodney King, himself, put a stop to it with his "Can't-we-all-just-get-along?" speech. Los Ange-les was still smoking on May 4, 1992, but I walked across that stage and received my bachelor's degree. There wasn't enough riot in the world to stop it. Five days later I was a graduate student. Little did I know that I was in for the challenge of my life, and the worst was yet to come.

thirty

I got off welfare.

A woman at USC's *Chronicle* wrote an article about me. Robin Abcarian at *Los Angeles Times* wrote an article about me. A few weeks later she wrote another article when her readers complained that they had worked three jobs and could not afford to send their kids to USC. Robin promptly admonished them and explained that an accomplishment like mine should be applauded, not looked upon with disdain.

All of a sudden I was in popular demand at women's groups and community colleges. The Los Angeles City Council gave me a resolution—a beautiful certificate that told my odyssey to L.A. Los Angeles City College honored me as its Outstanding Alumnus. Agents called about making a movie about my life. Television producers wanted me for talk shows, game shows, "exclusive" inside stories. For a minute I was caught up in the world of excitement. I did Bill Cosby's show, *You Bet Your Life.* I appeared on *The Les Brown Show* and *Hart to Heart,* and I did a five minute interview with Mary Major.

I was off welfare and everybody was happy about that. They could use me as an example. I could give hope to others and show them that it can be done. I could be an inspiration to other welfare mothers.

I was more than willing to do that, and I was good at it. I didn't expect anyone to try to do what I had done because maybe that wasn't what she wanted to do. But I could offer advice on how to find the help she needed. I could tell other women about books in the library that listed all kinds of scholarships. I could tell them to keep their kids involved so that their degree becomes a family project. I could tell them about getting to know one or two professors so that they will have something to say when they write a letter of recommendation.

I could help them stay in touch with the real world, too. At one of those meetings a young woman stood up and said, "Miz Lewis...I want to do exactly what you did...get scholarships, I mean. 'Cause I don't want no doggone loans."

I said, "What are you trying to tell me?"

"Ma'am?"

"Are you saying that you will terminate your education if you don't get a scholarship? Is that what you're trying to say?"

"Well… I just don't want to owe the federal government a whole lot of money."

I said, "Listen. If you buy a car, you're going to take out a loan. If you buy a house, you'll get a loan. You live in southern California where an earthquake, or a flood, or a fire or a riot can wipe out everything you own. But if you invest in your mind, until you die, you have an asset that no one can take away from you."

"I hadn't thought about it that way."

"Well, let me take it a step further. If you have to get a loan to finish school, it's better to borrow from the government because when you finish your schooling, all you owe them is money. If you borrow from a friend or your family, however, not only do you owe them money, you still owe the *favor*, and that is something you can never finish paying."

Clever. I patted my own back on that one.

I didn't realize how much I should have taken that advice for myself until Carolyn started acting funny. We had gone shopping to buy me an outfit to wear to my interview for Cosby's show. Nothing would satisfy Carolyn but to buy me some shoes to match. We couldn't find them on the first day, so we made an appointment to go to Nordstrom's. We got to the store and Carolyn took me to the shoe department and left me there. I found the perfect shoes within minutes, but Carolyn was nowhere to be found. After about fifteen minutes I had her paged.

She ran up to me in a huff. "What's the matter?"

"I found these great shoes!"

"So?"

"So I thought that's why we came."

"Well, I was shopping! For *me!*"

"I'm sorry."

"Well, never mind, now."

I had tried on three pairs. She scooped them all up and ran to the counter. The cashier was busy with another customer. Carolyn demanded to be waited on right away. The woman ignored her.

I had never seen Carolyn in such a state. She was drooling and shaky. She appeared to be very nervous. I said, "I don't need the shoes. Let's go."

Carolyn was absolutely livid. "It's because she's too lackadaisical to do her job. We were here first. It's because we're Black." She cut up for a while and a small crowd collected to watch the show. I kept trying to get her out of the store, but she said, "I'll get my husband to come up here. He will straighten this out." Carolyn's husband was a lawyer, a white lawyer. My thinking was that they looked at her and assumed that her husband was a big, violent Black guy, but one who offered no real threat to their business, so the clerk said to Carolyn, "Ma'am would you please shut up!"

That drove her wild; she demanded to see the manager immediately. By the time he got to us Carolyn was so angry she could hardly speak. Tears moistened her eyes. The manager asked what he could do to satisfy her, and I think she wanted the clerk fired on the spot. She never said that, though, and the matter was not resolved. She insisted on paying for the shoes, but when we left that store, Carolyn had changed.

During the drive home I said, "We didn't have to buy those shoes. I'm not even sure I want them now."

She said, "The shoes aren't the problem. I wanted you to have them. She kicked my ass in there. I entered a debate for which I was completely unprepared. I'll talk to Matthew. Next time I'll be better armed." Then she laughed. "I just wasn't ready," she said.

About ten o'clock that night I called Carolyn and asked her how she felt. She said, "Fine. The bitch got me." But I could hear Matthew in the background: "What did Miss Ford Fellow say? I'll bet she didn't open her mouth because she wanted those shoes." Carolyn said, "It wasn't anything Barbara could have said or done. I started it. It was my fight."

We talked until midnight, laughing it off. When we hung up the phone the last thing Carolyn said to me was, "Don't worry about it. It wasn't your fault."

Seven o'clock the next morning Carolyn called me.

"Barbara. I figured out what happened yesterday."

"You did? What?"

"I was Rodney King, and you were one of those cops standing around watching me get beat up. You never gave a damn about me. All you ever cared about was the money."

"That's not true—"

"Don't even try it!" and she hung up.

I tried to call her back, but no one answered the phone. I called every day, three or four times a day. After about a month I gave up. Then, towards the end of August, Matthew called and said that Carolyn had gone to Alabama. He said she told him that she had figured it all out. Said her name wasn't Rody; it was Rode-Y, and she had to go to Alabama to find out why the white people were killing up all the Black children. He said to me, "There are things going on that you don't know about. I think she really is crazy."

I told you all that to show that I took a lot of baggage to graduate school. I had lost what I considered to be my best friend. Los Angeles had become increasingly violent since the riots and gang wars and gun fights happened nearly every week. The language in the academy was altogether different from what I knew, and I thought to myself: *Oh God! I'm in the wrong place. I'm a fraud. They're going to find out and take the money away. How will I feed my kids?*

On top of all that, in my senior year of college, my sister had called to say that Jr. had a "spot" on his brain. I called him and he told me that the doctor said he didn't need an operation; he could get treatment as an outpatient. So, in September of 1992, I visited with him briefly when I went to Philadelphia for the Cosby show. He was in great spirits, but his wife told me that the "spot" was actually a tumor that was inoperable. And terminal.

At the end of my first year of graduate work I went to teach a summer course at the University of Oregon. When I returned to L.A., my sister-in-law called and said my brother was asking for me. The kids and I took a bus to New Jersey. We stayed there five weeks. When I first got there, I hardly recognized the old man who lay on that bed. But he could still talk a little. He wanted to tell me that he loved me. I needed to tell him the same thing.

We were not close as kids. He was the pesky little brother who told on me every chance he got, and I resented having to share my things with him, especially my money, because our father would not give him a dime. So, as adults we had spoken harshly to each other much too often, just couldn't *set horses*, as Mama would say. Family stuff had a way of making us say things out loud that could hurt for a long time. But I always loved him. I always prayed for him. I kept him on my mind while I tried to study. It was hard for me to accept that my little brother was going to die, but I wanted to be with him when it happened. I tried to transfer to a nearby university. Rutgers, Princeton, NYU—none of them would talk to me because recruitment was over. Seton Hall would have taken me in right away, but Seton Hall didn't offer the Ph.D. Ford didn't pay for a terminal M.A.

I called Christine O'Brien at the National Research Council in Washington. They administer the Ford fellowships. I asked her if I could take a year off so that I could stay with my brother. What she said sounded rather cold at the time, but it made perfect sense later: "Is your brother going to die anyway?"

"Yes."

"Do you think he'd want you to put your life on hold for him?"

No. I did not think he'd want that. So, I went back to Los Angeles and started my second year of graduate work. Ten days after I got home my brother died. I had to turn right around and go back to New Jersey.

Jr.'s death brought new meaning to my life. For one thing, it put me in touch with my own mortality. For another, a part of my brain was set free. I no longer panicked when the phone rang. I no longer wondered how I would react to the news. I no longer had to worry about him dying. He was dead. His suffering was over.

At his funeral, the only thing anybody said about him was that he sang *The Lord's Prayer* very well. Nobody, not even his wife, said anything about the kind of man he was, the kind of ambitions he had, the plans he made or the things he accomplished in life. It occurred to me then that my dreams were not about empty vanity. I believed I had important work to do.

I guess I needed to clear that brain space so that I could function more effectively. There were a lot of things going on that required intense thought. Aside from my studies, my kids were in constant danger. Gang and drug violence threatened them at every corner in South Central. There was a shooting one evening at the park where my kids played baseball and basketball. They also went to camp there in the summers. Two people died at the scene; one of them was a man in a wheelchair who was watching television in his home. And the retaliation was something else again. All told, seven people died that night.

Drive-by shootings, point blank range, street fighting—it didn't matter. Too many young Black men were dying before they reached twenty-five, and I was afraid for my son all the time. I walked him to and from school. I took him to see his girlfriend and I stayed there. I watched him closely, even when he went across the street to the store. Oh, we went through some times about that. He thought I was trying to treat him like a baby. He said I was overly protective. He was old enough to experience life on his own, he said. But he was still my son and my job was to protect him, I said. It kept us at a tug of war and I'll admit, I was unyielding. He never disrespected me; he just tuned me out. So I would raise my voice to make sure he heard me even if he wasn't ready to process my message. I said he should be grateful that I cared enough to protect him. I did not tell him any of those *I walked seven miles in the snow just to get to school* stories, but I did tell him that Rodney King proved that not much had changed for Black people since I was a kid. I let him know that he was very fortunate; he did not have to go out and make his own way. I always had a lot of responsibility but no guidance. I had to take risks; he didn't. I had to figure things out for myself, and figuring things out got me into a whole lot of trouble.

I told my son about the night my daddy was sick and I had to go to the drugstore at one in the morning. I had been awake for a long time; nobody could sleep when Daddy was sick. He had suffered with ulcers as long as I'd known him, and on this particular night he had a really bad attack. It was cold in Wilson that night. The wind blew trash from the street that stuck to the plastic coverings on the windows. I had ironed my sheets to warm them, and I didn't dare move. An inch in any direction offered the threat of freezing while I lay there. Rain poured down outside and a steady drip— *ping, ping*—fell into the pan I had placed in my room where the heater used to be. I pushed myself farther under the covers and pretended to be asleep. I knew I would be the one who had to go to Terminal Drugstore.

Sure enough, Mama made a fire and came into my room to wake me. This is the kind of stuff I tried to tell my kids. If I had been my own mama, I would have defended my child. I would have told him that *he* should go to the store at one in the morning. I would have told him that it was twenty degrees outside with rain as hard as bullets. I would have reminded him that the child was only twelve. But Daddy cussed and threw the Bible past Mama's ear and I was off and running. Mama thrust a dollar in one hand, an umbrella in the other, and I ran out the front door into the cold, the rain and the dark.

The fastest route from our house was to go down Viola Street, up Vick Street, turn right and take Green Street all the way past the railroad tracks. Then, turn left at the bus station, pass the train station and cross Nash Street. The drugstore was on the corner.

I ran all the way. The streets were unusually dark that night. The rain came towards the front of me in torrents. I positioned my umbrella to cover my face; the rain poured down the back of my neck. The cold had teeth that nibbled at my ears. A dog chased me and I ran harder. When I was no longer a threat to his territory he turned back. The wind howled and seemed to whisper my name—Barb'raah…Barb'raah… By the time I reached the store I was out of breath and I had to pee. But there was no time for that. I could still hear my daddy cussing and I wondered if Mama and Jr. were all right.

Terminal Drugstore stayed open all night and it doubled as a café for white folks. For a moment I stood outside the store trying to catch my breath. Through the glass doors I could see the people inside laughing and talking, smoking cigarettes and drinking coffee. The pharmacist stood at his counter talking to a woman with blond hair and heavy thighs. I entered the store and all motion stopped. The only noise I could hear was the squish of my wet tennis shoes against the tile floor. The heat in the room made me nauseous and my mouth filled up with sweet, hot spit. I swallowed the vomit in my throat and walked steadily towards the counter. I could feel their eyes staring at me. As I walked, everything to the right and left of me grew dark. The pharmacist seemed very far away. There was a flood of light surrounding him. I stretched my eyes to adjust to the brightness, but the closer I got to him, the brighter he became. It was a hot, white light, and looking at him was like looking through the wrong end of a telescope.

At last I reached the counter. I stood there holding my wet dollar in my fist, and I waited for the man in the gleaming white coat to say, "May I help you?" The urge to pee persisted and I squeezed my thighs together. Glancing around the room I saw that all those white people were looking at me. They knew I had to pee. They knew I was not allowed to sit down. I was convinced that the pharmacist understood my predicament as well. That's why he prolonged waiting on me. The caustic vomit returned to my throat and I opened my mouth as if to speak.

"Waal," the man in the white coat said. "Whutcha wont gal?"

I cleared my throat and placed the wet dollar on the counter.

"Bisodol."

The bottom of my stomach ached and I thought my bladder would explode. The pharmacist continued his conversation with the heavy-thighed lady, and the people inside the store resumed their chatter. I wanted to run. I started crying. Mama would whip me for sure if I peed on myself in front of all these white people.

Finally the druggist handed me my package. He put the change in the bag. "Now git!" he said, and I made a quick dash for the door. The laughter of the folks inside followed me out into the cold night air. It had stopped raining. I ran across the street to the restroom at the train station. Clutching my bag and umbrella with one hand and my crotch with the other, I could tell that the hot liquid had already begun to trickle. I tried the door marked "COLORED;" it was locked. I searched the grounds for a bush or tree large enough to hide me. There was none. I spotted the sign that read, "WHITE LADIES ONLY." In desperation I opened the door and went in.

I peed for a long time. As I finished using the toilet and was about to leave, I heard the door open. Two white women came in. I checked the lock on the stall door. It was secure. Panic raced through my blood. I pulled my feet up on the seat and waited for them to go away. My heart pounded so hard I could feel the vibrations in my ears. The thought that they might hear it terrified me.

One of the women tried the door. "Is enybody in thar?" she asked.

"Uh huh," I grunted.

"Waal, yew gonna be in thar long?"

I tried to imitate the way white people talked. "Yeh-is," I said, forcing a strain. "Ah'm see-ick."

The women loitered for a few moments and then decided to go across the street. Hearing the quiet, I ran out of there as fast as I could.

When I returned home my mother was pacing the floor. "Where've you been? You've been gone two hours! Your daddy went looking for you."

I started telling her the story while she helped me get out of my wet clothes. When I reached the part about the two white ladies in the restroom, I realized I had left the medicine there.

Just then I heard Daddy's footsteps on the front porch. My heart jumped. He opened the door and stood there, dripping wet. I thought of hiding behind Mama, but that wouldn't keep him away from me. I moved closer to the stove, my whole body trembling—partly from cold, partly from the rain, but mostly from fear of what Daddy would do to me.

"Come heah," he said.

"Now, Wiley—"

Daddy pointed his finger at the floor. "I said, 'Come heah.'"

I walked towards him. He reached for me and I ducked. He grabbed me by the shoulder and lifted me under the arms. For the first time in my life I was face to face with my daddy. Though it had stopped raining, his face was wet. His eyes were wet. They were light brown, and I could see my image in them.

"You all right?"

"Yes, Sir."

He clenched his teeth and I could see his temples move up and down. Gazing into each other's eyes he slowly lowered me to the floor and we all went back to bed.

So, as I told my son that story, I realized that, in their own way, my parents loved me. But their way was not my way. "The kind of child I was needed the kind of parent I am," I told him.

Parenting didn't come with a blueprint. I told my son that story thinking that it would make him understand my need to protect him, but I was not the kind of parent he needed at that time, and it just about killed me when he said, "I want to go stay with my daddy, man."

I made no effort to send him to Ronald. Instead I decided to loosen the reins just a little bit. I let him go to the store by himself. I'd take him to his girl's house and leave him there. Once, I even let him go to a movie with some friends. And then one day, my son was robbed at gunpoint.

He had just turned fourteen and he wanted to go to the barber shop alone.

He had earned ten dollars babysitting and I gave him five. He said, "I'm old enough, Mama. I'm almost a man." So I said a prayer and sent him on his way. He had to walk five blocks west to Western and one block north. But he was back in less than twenty minutes. It was Wednesday. I laughed at him.

"Somebody who is almost a man ought to know the schedule. The barber shop was closed, right?"

"Naw. I got jacked Ma."

I grabbed my baby who was almost a man and squeezed him tightly while I thanked God for bringing him home. I cried for a long time, and he cried because I cried. Then he told me the story:

I was walking past Foshay when I noticed these two dudes across the street. They walked up on me and one of 'em said, "Hey man…lemme hold sumpin." I said, "I ain't got no money." The dude said, "Well where you goin'?" I said, "To the barber shop." The other dude said, "How you gonna go to the barber shop if you ain't got no ends?" And then the first dude hit me 'cross the back of my head. I swung at him and hit him in the mouth. The other dude reached behind his jacket and said, "Hey man, I got heat," and pulled out a gun. I threw my hands up and they took my fifteen dollars. Then the janitor came out of Foshay and said, "Hey! What's going on here? And the dudes ran away. He paused for a second and squeezed my hand. Mama…I could feel that hole in my head. I could see myself laying on the sidewalk with my brains pouring out and you didn't know where I was.

After that he didn't seem to mind that I went with him everywhere, but there was a change in him. He was angry and aggressive. He didn't walk away from an argument at school anymore. He'd say things like, "I ain't afraid of nothing! 'Specially no punk ass niggers. They scared of me. That's why they stay strapped."

I didn't know it at the time, but he had been threatened in school every day. The problem? He had finished middle school at Foshay. Foshay was in a blue area and he should have gone to Manual Arts for high school. But he wanted to play football for Dorsey, and Dorsey was predominantly a red school. The Bloods at Dorsey apparently thought he was a Crip because he came from Foshay. They'd gather around him at lunch time and tell him what they planned to do to him and his family.

This went on for about a week before he told me about it. Trying to be a man, you know. I immediately called Ronald. We agreed that our son could move in with him and his wife in North Carolina.

179

Putting my son on that plane and watching him leave were the hardest things I have ever had to do. It left me with a sick feeling in the pit of my stomach. He had been my rock, my anchor for so long. Once, for example, when he was twelve, I earned a 'B' in a course I had taken in graduate school. The grade was based on the final paper and I had put all I had into that paper. I walked all the way home in a kind of funk, and when I got there, my son waited for me by the fence. He took one look at my face and said, "Oh Lord, Mama. What in the world is the matter?" I let go then, and I fell into his arms and cried. He comforted me and assured me that I could get over the 'B' and move forward. Finally he said, "Mama, if I got a 'B' in English, I would cry, too, but they would be tears of joy." That's the kind of man he would become, always capable of making one feel better about him or herself.

For days after he left I received threatening phone calls: *What's up Blood? What's up Cuz? We gon' git you nigger!* But as I look back on it, I believe that decision saved my son's life.

I think about that now and I get angry. The Bloods and the Crips. The Harpies and the Chollos. The 18th Street gang. The 60s. The 30s. The 20s. Asian gangs. Mexican Mafia. Damn it all. They mark off territories and kill anyone who disrespects them by wearing the wrong color. They don't own shit. Yet, they claim that territory as if it were their own. It would be different if they protected their neighborhoods, but they are just as violent towards their own as they are against their enemies.

It seems to me that the gangs do the supremacist's work for him. They eliminate each other and *the man* keeps his hands clean. That was the painful part. After the King beating, I had to explain to my son that he was a Black man, and that automatically made him a suspect. A man of color is at great risk in cities like L.A. If the gangs don't get him, the cops will. Half the time these killings don't even make it to the media; they are dismissed as "gang-related." Another Black man dies; another Black mother cries, and I resented having to tell him that.

Los Angeles had been very good to me. That's the truth. One day I hope to do something wonderful for that city to pay it back, but I was unwilling to sacrifice my only son to the streets of L.A. So, I sent him to live with a man he didn't even know: his father.

thirty-one

SHIT HAPPENS.

That was a logo that I saw on a tee shirt one day and I searched all over town before I found it and bought it. Those two words said everything I wanted to say then. They say what I want to say to you now. When you are in graduate school, things happen that make you realize that life exists beyond the academy. People die. Friendships disintegrate. Deadlines have to be met. Children have to be loved, nurtured, encouraged. Trouble is ubiquitous.

The first time I heard that word *ubiquitous,* it was uttered by Dr. Ronald Gottesman. It was in a seminar on violence, and in his opening lecture Ron said, "Violence is ubiquitous." He talked about the violence upon which this country was founded. We discussed war and riots, domestic violence, racial and sexual violence. We also talked about psychic violence and the damage it can do. In that class I learned everything I needed to know about surviving graduate school. Under Ron's tutelage, and through his eyes, I discovered who I really am. I realized my strengths and weaknesses, and I became acutely aware of the effects of psychic violence on me.

I still had a tendency to internalize guilt. Whenever things happened that altered my plans, I tried to ignore them or wish them away. I'd go to sleep and hope that things would be better in the morning. I was like Anne Bradstreet in that regard; if things were not perfect, I figured that God was punishing me for something I had done.

But even I realized that the punishment was severe. It didn't affect only me; my children had to suffer for decisions I had made. I received a letter from the District Attorney. It threatened to cut off my welfare check if I did not come to court to testify against Kwame for child support. When the baby was born, Kwame had begged me to put his name on her birth certificate. He had wanted a child; I did not want to write in the "father" block: *Unknown.* So we agreed to put his name there. Since I had not seen him in twelve years, I saw no need to concern myself with him now. Besides, I was no longer on welfare, so the DA's threat meant nothing to me. I ignored the notice.

Another letter came telling me to take my child for a blood test. I ignored that one, too. Then, finally, I got a subpoena to go to court. I went to see the DA on the day before the court date. I explained to him that I didn't even know Kwame, that I was new to the city when the child was conceived and that I had been raped.

"We'll have to reschedule this," he said to me. "He denies being the father. You have to take the child to Long Beach and get a blood test for both of you."

"Didn't you hear what I just said? I don't want to be near him. You can't make me do this," I said. "I am not on welfare anymore, and I don't want my child subjected to some stupid blood test."

"Well, the judge can make you do it. If you're telling me right now that you are not going to go, I'll take you in to see the judge. He'll make you do it, or you'll go to jail for contempt!"

I needed some time to decide what to do, so I stalled and told him that I would go to Long Beach. All kinds of things went through my mind. My daughter was eleven years old. She didn't know anything at all about Kwame. She assumed that Henry was her father because he found us one day when he had his little boy with him. His boy and my girl were both two, and the boy called him "Daddy." My little girl picked up on that right away and she called Henry "Daddy," too. I didn't do or say anything to stop it because it was, after all, *convenient.* Now, though, how could I tell her that Henry may not be her father? How could I tell her that I had lied to her all those years? How, pray tell, do you tell an eleven year old girl that her father is a rapist?

I hired a lawyer. That bought me some time. It cost me four hundred dollars, but it bought the time I needed to decide what I should say to my child. I did not want to testify in court. I did not want to be in the same room with him. But it looked like I couldn't avoid a confrontation, so I took my baby for a walk and told her everything. She didn't seem to have any reaction, so I asked her, "What do you think?"

"About what?"

"About what I just told you."

"Nothing."

"Nothing? Surely you must be thinking something."

"Not really."

"You mad?"

"At who?"

"Me."

"No! Why should I be mad at you?"

"Because I let you believe that Henry was your father."

"I don't care about that. I don't even like him."

"Well, what do you care about?"

"I care about you. You always told me that I was your daughter. Said I was God's gift to you. You still feel that way?"

"Absolutely!"

"Then what's the problem?"

"The problem is that the DA wants you to take a blood test because the other guy says he is not your father."

"Blood test?"

"Yes."

"Needles?!"

"Yes, well, one anyway."

"No. I don't want to do that."

"Then I'll make sure that you don't have to."

The answer was so simple. I don't know why I didn't think of it before. I went to the courthouse and found the DA. He was furious.

"Look, Ms. Lewis. I am losing my patience with you! We still don't have a record of your blood test. You are wasting the taxpayers' money and my precious time!"

I was so together that day. I stared him straight in the eye. "That man is not my child's father."

"What?!" He looked like his tie was suddenly too tight, and he turned bright red in the face.

"I said…that man is not my child's father. I will sign an affidavit to that effect."

"Women like you make me sick!" he said. You've tied this thing up for months. And this poor man…"

I signed a handwritten note and got the hell out of there. I could not escape Kwame, however. He caught up with me outside the courthouse. I did not want to talk to him.

"Leave me alone. Please."

"Wait. I need to explain."

"I don't need an explanation. I just need you to leave me alone."

"But I have to tell you."

I had to wait for the bus. I knew he would continue to pester me if I didn't listen to him, and that would be dangerous because I really wanted to knock the shit out of him. "Okay. What?"

"I would be very happy to be her father, but I don't have any money. At first I only complained about the child support, but then the DA told me that you were going to file a rape charge against me. I'm trying to get into medical school. I can't have a charge like that on my record."

"Are you finished?"

"Yes, but listen. Maybe I could see her sometime. I really would like to be her father."

"No thanks. You stay away from my child." The bus came and I boarded without looking back.

Shit happens.

Weird shit. A man stripped down to his baby blue shorts and started directing traffic at the corner of Normandy and Exposition. He climbed the lamp pole and pledged allegiance to an invisible flag. The cops brought him down, cuffed his wrists and ankles and chained them all together. Then they threw him face down into the back seat of the squad car.

Dumb shit. A man came to my door one day and tried to sell me a car battery for forty dollars. I told him I already had one. Later that day, when I was rushing off to campus, I turned the key and nothing happened. I looked under the hood and discovered it was my own battery that he had tried to sell to me.

Dangerous shit. A gold Mercedes drove slowly past the apartment building across the street and opened fire. My kids were outside playing. I ran to the door and yelled, "Get in here! Get on the floor!" When it was over I looked around the room and took inventory. Twenty-two children were in my house. I didn't even know a dozen of them.

Irresponsible shit. With everything else that was going on in my life, I found myself worrying about money. It wasn't that I had overspent my budget; it was the red tape involved in generating my check. I didn't have the money to overspend. That was my only problem at USC. My fellowship monies were in place in September of each year, but there was only one person who had the authority to issue my check every month. If she was on vacation, out sick or had some other reason to be absent, I was stuck with no money until she returned.

The first time it happened was at Thanksgiving of 1992. It happened again at Christmas. Before I finished my graduate studies, it happened a dozen times. She simply did not set her computer to distribute my check before she left. But I had found a friend in Ron Gottesman. He was the one professor at USC who took the time to get to know me. He didn't try to mold me into something I wasn't; he just listened to me and helped me develop the woman I was.

He was also a very sensitive human being. At one point in the violence seminar, a colleague asked the question, "Where were you when JFK was shot?" My memory of that horrible day brought tears to my eyes. I covered my face and bowed my head. When I looked up, Ron was crying, too.

Ron understood my concern for my children. In the middle of a seminar, if we heard a siren, he would suggest that I go call my kids. He understood and encouraged my drive to do everything at one time. I once told him that I wanted to read everything Toni Morrison had ever written, and when she won the Nobel Prize he said to me in front of the whole class: "Well, Barbara, you sure know how to pick 'em."

He advised me on every single issue, and I followed that advice to the letter. I also followed him. Whenever I saw him on campus I'd run to catch up with him just to talk. He knew so much about everything, and I believed I could absorb knowledge just by breathing in the same air he did. One day I caught him in the hallway just after he had finished a class. I charged towards him and started asking questions. He answered, of course, but he kept walking. When he turned a corner, I turned a corner. Finally, he stopped and said to me, "Barbara, what is the strongest letter in the alphabet?" I was bewildered. I quickly said, "I don't know." And he said, "Pee! Because you can't hold it." It was then that I noticed I was about to follow him into the men's room.

I can honestly say that without Ron Gottesman I might have been lost. There were many times when I sat down and asked myself, *Is it worth all this?* Ron assured me that it was.

Most of those times were related to my feeling of powerlessness because I had no money. So, in December of 1995, when I went to pick up my check only to discover that it was not there, I went to see Ron. I was already expecting to spend Christmas without my son; that hurt, but I could deal with it. But I had ten job interviews lined up in Chicago at the Modern Language Association conference; I needed my money. I felt like the world was falling apart around me. I said to him, "Maybe I slapped my mama in a previous life. I don't understand why I have so much trouble. I believe I am doing the right thing. Goddammit! I *know* I am doing the right thing, but why does it have to be so difficult?"

He said, "That's because you are getting ready to win. You always have hard times just before a victory."

Ron made one phone call—just one, and I had my check by the end of the day. It was never late again.

Author's Note

THIS IS THE STORY I wanted to share with my classmates during our reunion. When Gloria's husband died, however, it seemed inappropriate to try to focus their attention in my direction. But I wanted, I *needed* to tell someone, and talking with you like this has been extremely beneficial. I feel so much better. I know I have given you a lot to ponder. I have heard you laugh with me. I have seen you cry for me. You might even have a few questions that I have not answered. Some of them have no answers. As for the others, well, perhaps we'll talk again.

I don't know what happened between my son and his father. I don't really care to know. He had left my house in October, 1995 and he was back in March, 1996. By that time I had almost finished my dissertation. I taught two classes at City College in the fall of that school year, and two classes at Cal State Northridge in the spring. I wrote my book in nine months. I had determined to get my Ph.D. before I ran out of funding. I had also decided to take a position at The University of Texas in Austin. That put me on the fast track.

I home-schooled my son for the rest of the year. It was a lot of work, but at least I knew he was safe.

Ron had previously announced that he would no longer chair dissertation committees; he was very busy organizing his thoughts about his own project: an encyclopedia about violence in America. I asked him anyway. I told him that I wanted to do a study on Toni Morrison, Zora Neale Hurston and other famous African American women writers. I even had a name for my project: *Prodigal Daughters: Female Heroes, Fugitivity and 'Wild' Women.* He loved the title and he wrote me a note: "I am sure to learn something along the way."

The good news about having Ron Gottesman for my chair was that he did not try to make me write what he wanted to read; instead, he gave me the freedom to be expressive on the issues that concerned me. He trusted me enough to let me write at my own pace. Most importantly, Ron and his wife, Beth, helped me through those last few months in more ways than I can articulate. On the day of graduation, Ron strutted me through USC's campus. Beth fixed my hood. They understood me and my need to be recognized at the end of this particular journey. They threw a big party to celebrate my accomplishments.

On the day of my defense—on that glorious day—I thought about green Packards and bicycles and scooters and roller skates. I kicked off my shoes. I bowed my head. And Ron Gottesman was the first to shake the hand of Dr. Barbara Williams Lewis.

Getting my Ph. D. only started the healing process; I still have a long way to go. When the announcement of my doctorate appeared in *The Wilson Daily Times,* my mother called me. She said, "I'm so proud of you I don't know what in the world to do. Now, all you need is a man, and I don't care what color he is 'cause I ain't color struck," and for a moment I began to see myself as a whole lot of good woman gone to waste. I tried to explain to her that if it were a husband I wanted, I could have kept every one of those I had. But the wounds were too deep, and every time I tried to start a new relationship, I found myself picking at old involvements. The scabs of those sores continued to re-open and re-infect themselves.

So, you see, while I might not look like it, scars remain. Some of them are permanent. I am not nearly as anti-marriage as I used to be; every once in a while I think about the comforts of having a man around and I try to believe that a good one waits for me. But because of Hubbie and Ronald and Henry and Kwame and Achmed, I don't even make eye contact with men anymore. I keep myself knee-deep in my work because I came to realize that there is something in me that attracts the wrong kind of man. It was there all along. I'm not exactly sure what it is, but until I can put my finger on it, until I can finish healing, it is better for me to remain single.

I hope you've learned something from all this, especially you women who are on welfare and those of you who are victims of domestic violence. Yes. Especially you. And some men, too. I see you all on the street. I recognize the terror in your eyes. I talk to you even when you reject me, because it is my job. It is an appointment made by the universe.

My education does not mean that I know everything. In fact, I've come to realize that in terms of the world, I know very little. As long as I can read I can continue to learn, and this is what I have learned thus far: My abuser did not love me. He hated me because he needed me. I could never change that hate. I could not cure that fear. The only thing I could do was get out and find my own personal freedom.

As I learn, I teach. I gave my dissertation its title because I see myself in every aspect of it. I think we are all fugitives in some form or another; each of us runs away from something. But as an old man once said to me, "It ain't the leaving, it's the coming back that hurt me so bad." That's true. Sometimes we have to become prodigal and distant and then take inventory of what we have learned. Then we have to give up the prodigality before we can move forward. We have to go back to what Morrison calls our "original place."

One of my earliest memories is about separation, dislocation. At three I experienced a separation from my mother that caused me a lot of anguish because I was not prepared for it. This writing, then, is my attempt to go there and unlock and discard all the garbage I've picked up along the way. I have had to re-invent myself and create a life of uninhibited freedom.

This, then is my advice to you. I promise you that it won't be easy; there will always be an obstacle in your way. But you have to decide to be a winner. You have to decide what makes you happy, what makes you whole. All too often we let somebody else define happiness for us, and then we only *look* happy. We are still enslaved by someone else's standards.

I've learned a lot about the system, too. It seems to me that if one is on welfare and escapes, the system tries to bring her back down. It took a long time for me to get ahead because the DA and other bureaucrats kept reminding me that I owed them. Yet, they were unwilling to let me pay. Money is not what they want. Our complete dehumanization is. It is a double jeopardy. They punish us for needing them by regulating everything except how many times we use the toilet. But if we get out, they punish us for not needing them by reminding us that we needed them in the first place. As James Baldwin says on page eleven of *Another Country,* "This shit is got to stop!" Poverty is not a crime.

I implore you to share my story with a friend. Go deep inside and discover who you are and then share it with a friend. I know that you know someone who could use a little help. I had to arm myself with the artillery I needed; you should, too. I don't mean that you should go out and buy a firearm; violence does not solve violence. My weapon of choice was reading good books. Through books I discovered that others are aware of certain issues that directly affect me, a woman.

I've learned something else, too. Shakespeare writes about unrequited love; I have unrequited anger. Unrequited disgust. I could have been a murderer, a thief, a con artist, a *ho,* a drug addict. Everything in my environment indicated a life of crime and an early death. I chose to be different.

That notion is something I got from another book. Jean Paul Sartre writes that we have to be responsible for ourselves. We have to choose our own path and take responsibility for that choice. He says that even when we don't choose we are still choosing because we choose not to choose. That makes sense now. I used to take on the burdens of the non-choosers. I tried to make everything right for them. Now I have learned that I have just enough breath for one life. *Mine.* I am going to do everything I can to get this one right. I will never again let someone else tell me what I cannot do. I set my own goals. I have no limitations. I can jump at the sun. I can ride the air. I can smile at a rainbow, especially the one for colored girls. I can cherish a scrub board, appreciate a brownstone, play in a mud puddle, dance in the rain. I can admire the color purple without thinking about bruises. I can color outside the lines. I can touch, taste, smell, see, feel and hear my own history. I can even rewrite it if I want to. I can walk through hell and drink ice water. Believing *that*…cushions the bumpy road to enlightenment. I have got to keep on keeping on. For me.

Yes. Scars remain. I do not have a tree on my back the way Sethe does. I do, however, have a tree in *my* back. It may bend, and it may sway, but it will never break. Surrender is fatal.